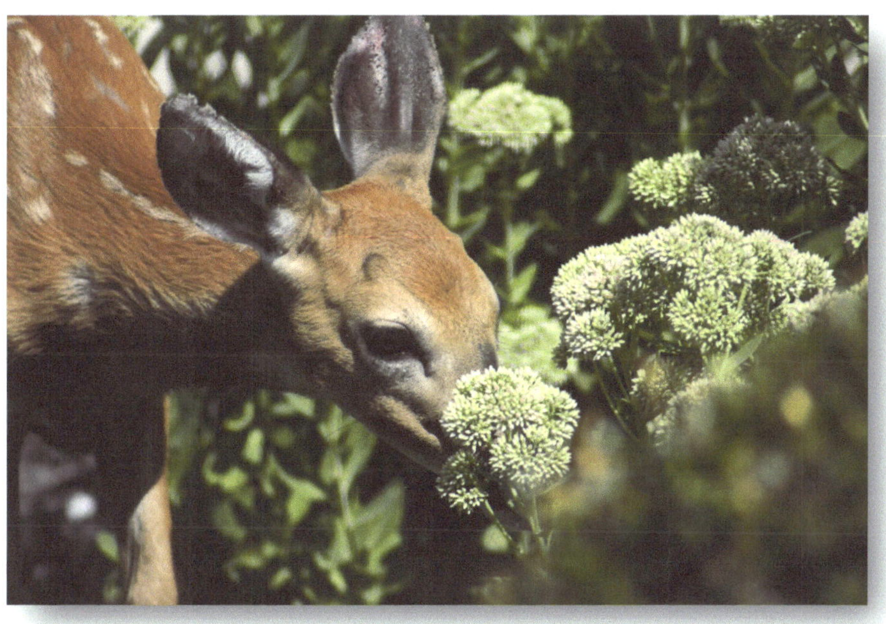

Virginia Wildlife

Tracey Hughes

***

***

***

***

Deep Sea Publishing ISBN: 1939535026
Deep Sea Publishing ISBN-13: 978-1-939535-02-3

***

www.deepseapublishing.com

***

Printed in the United States of America

DEDICATION

Psalms 104:24

Credit belongs to the one who created the amazing variety of creatures big and small, Our Creator, Our God, Our Lord and Savior. In capturing these creatures in any art form is all anyone can do because we do not create the beauty, just pass it on. Take the time, be still, and observe. He made it for us all.

-Tracey Y. Hughes

Deer

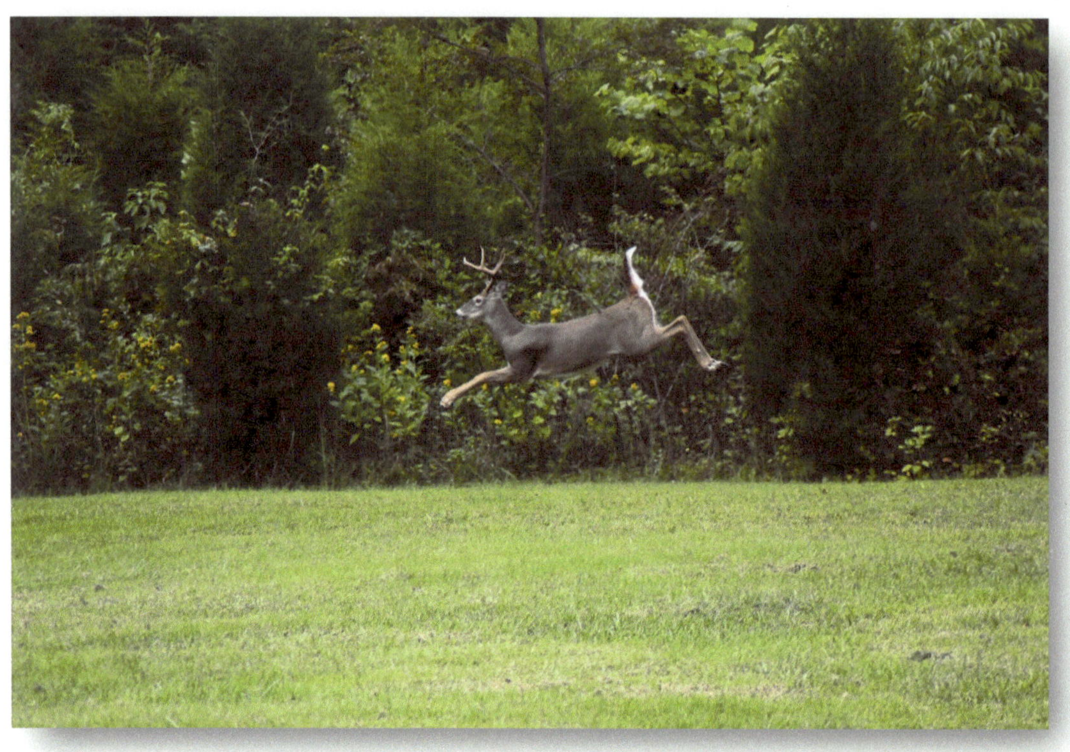

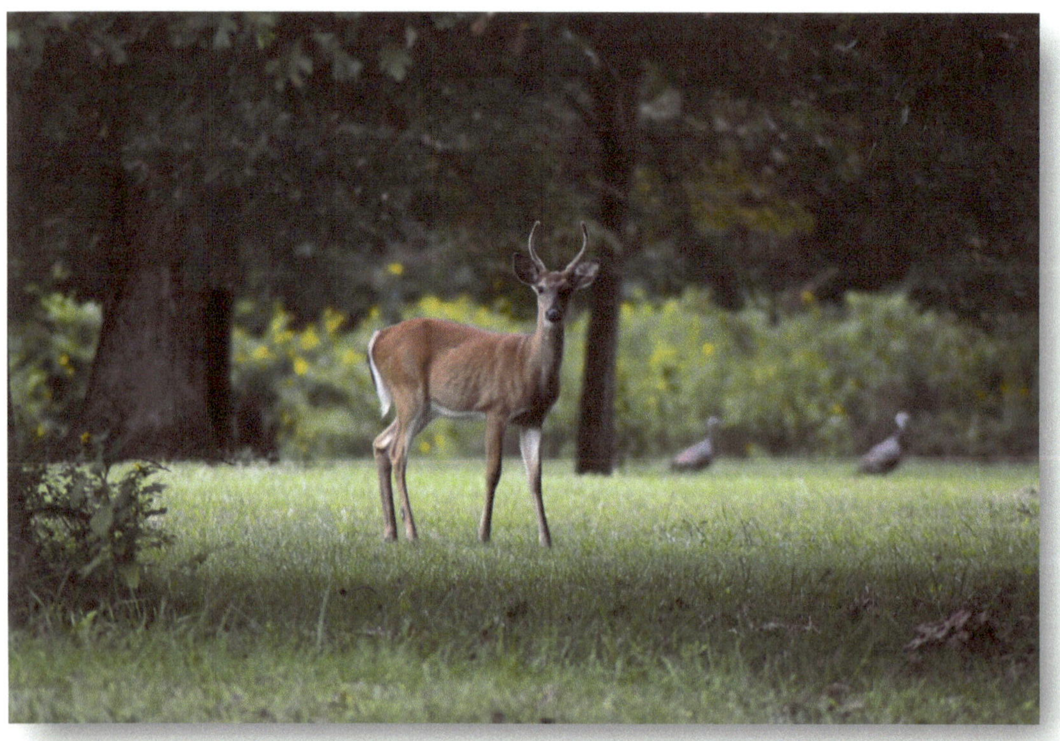

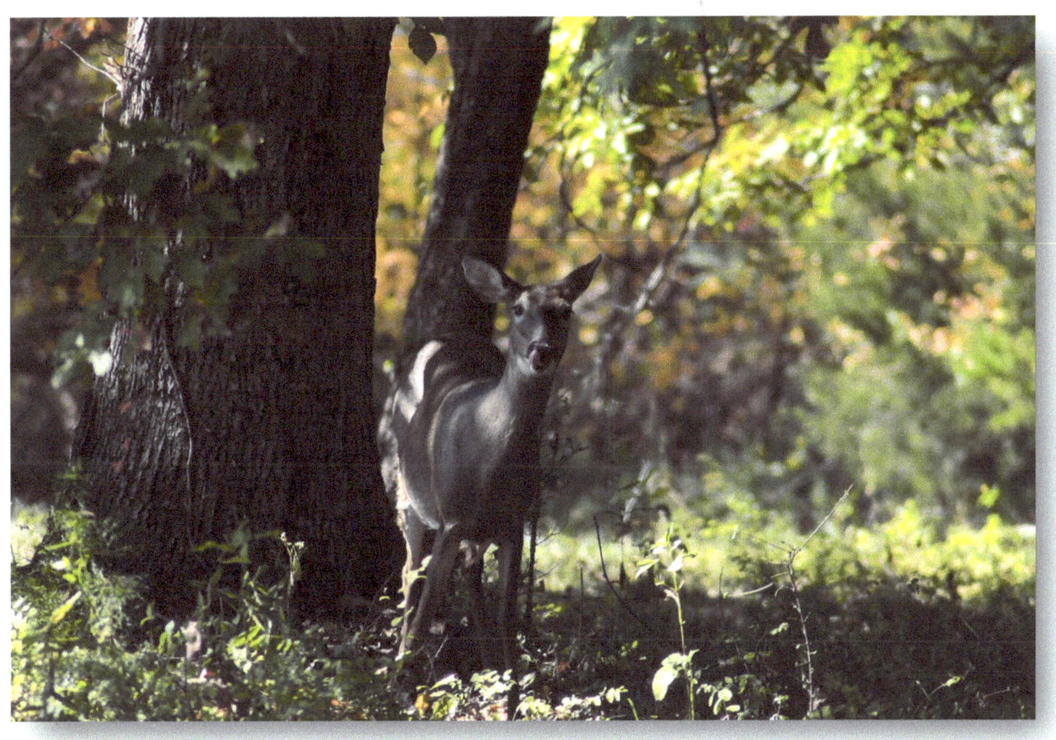

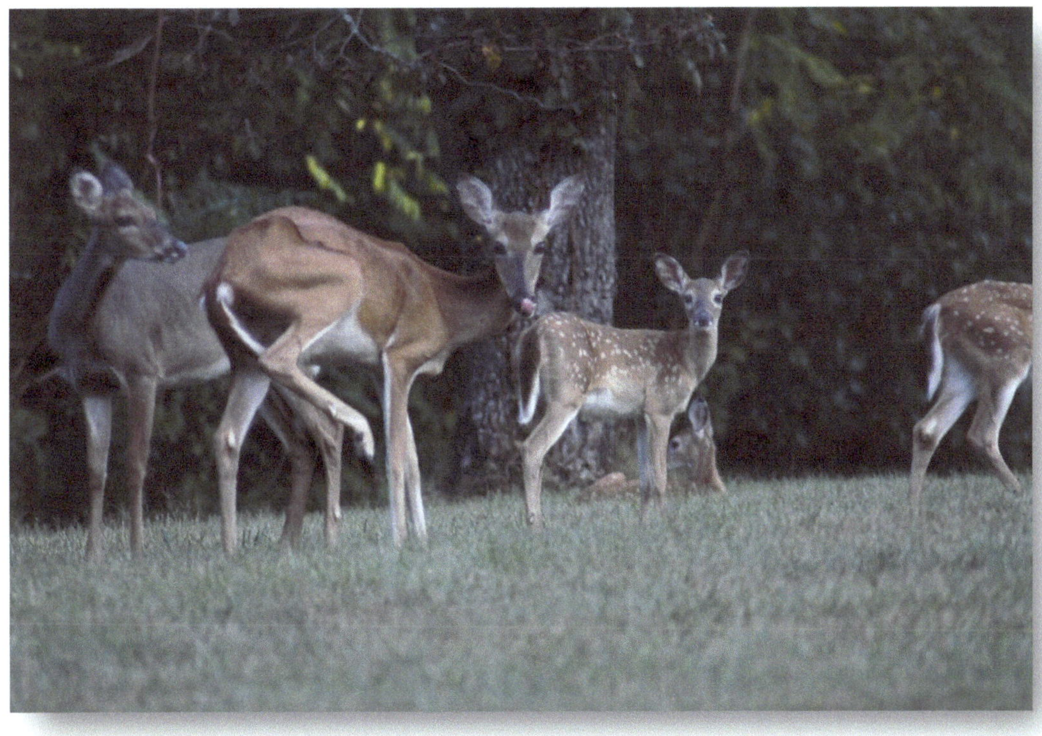

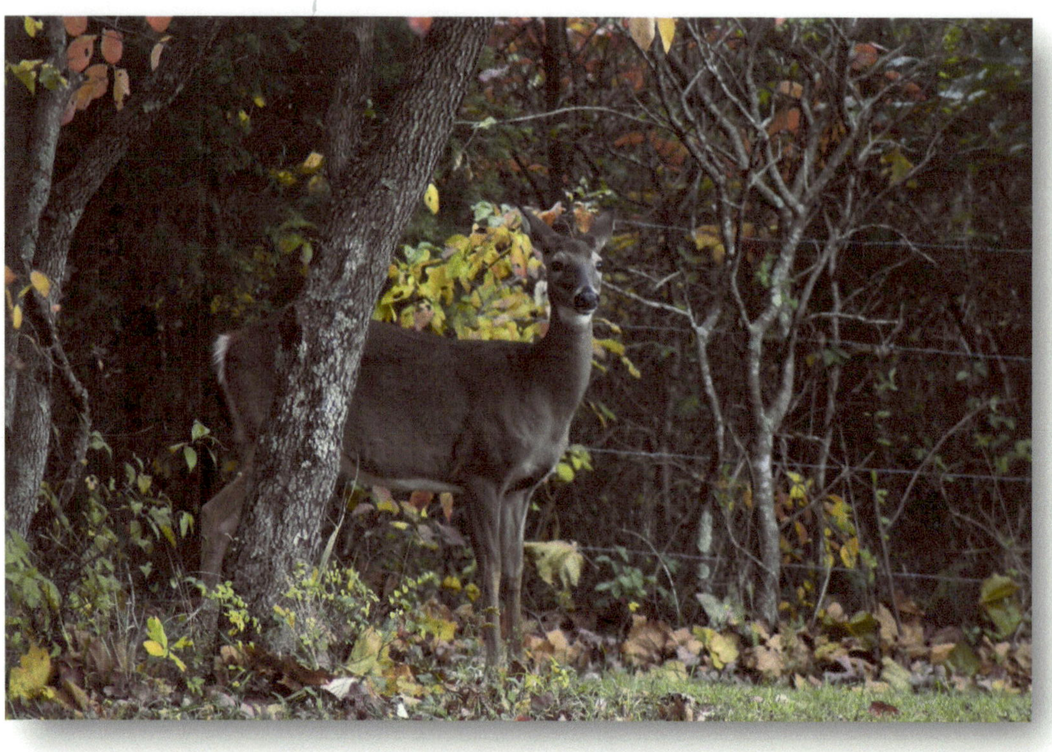

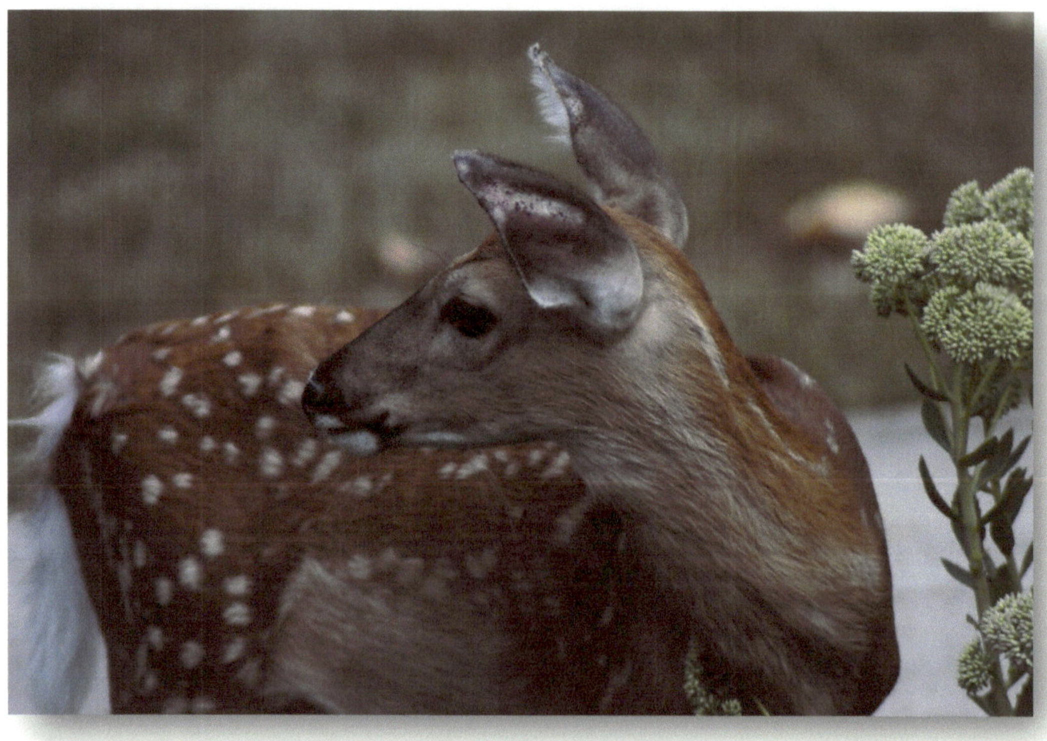

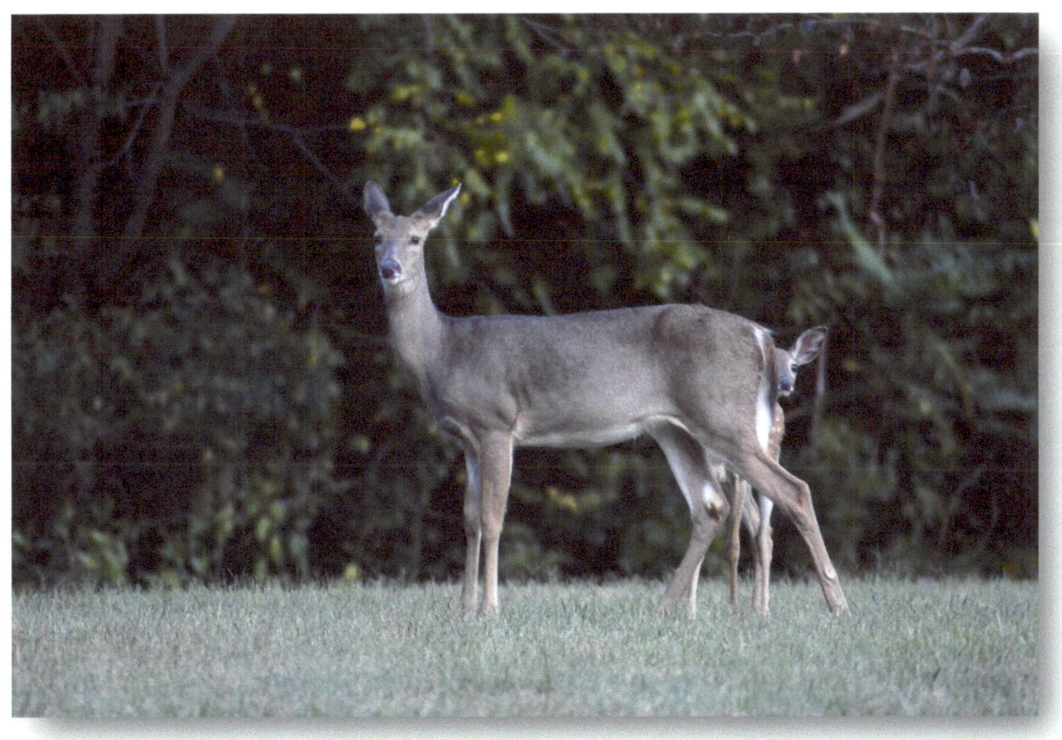

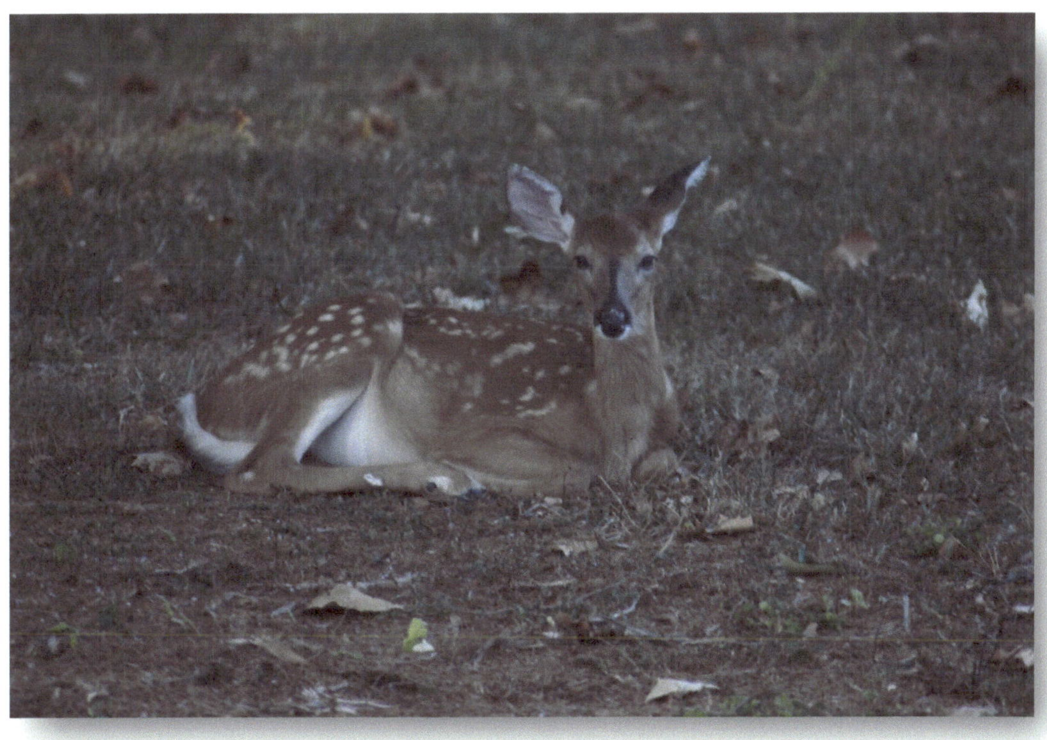

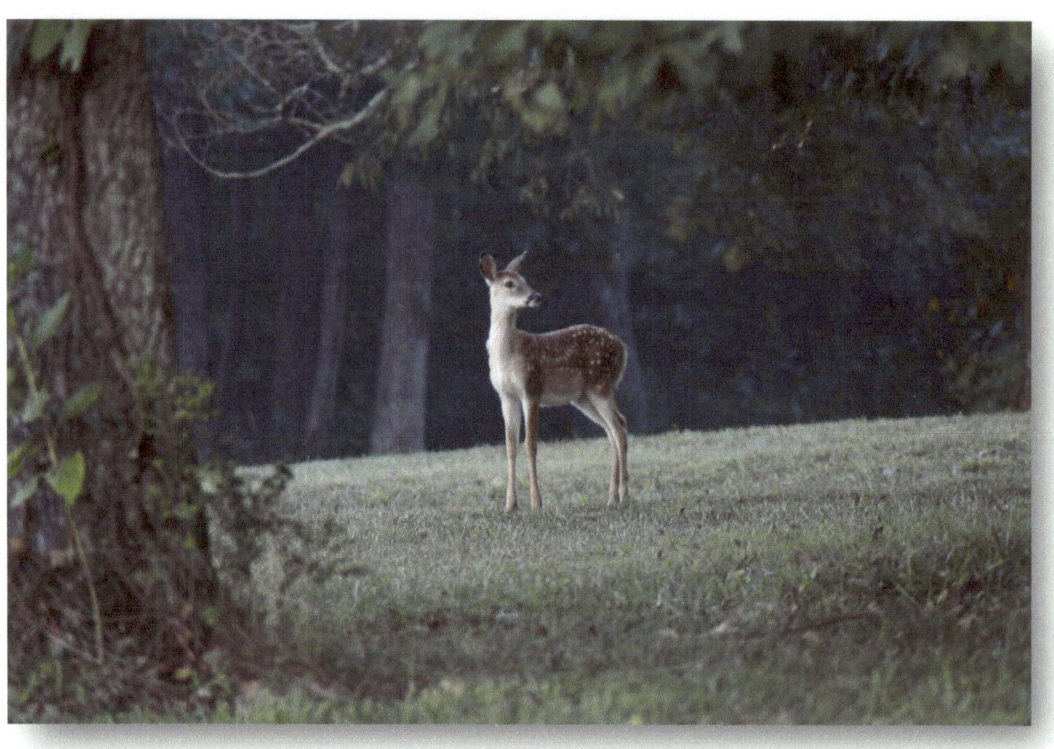

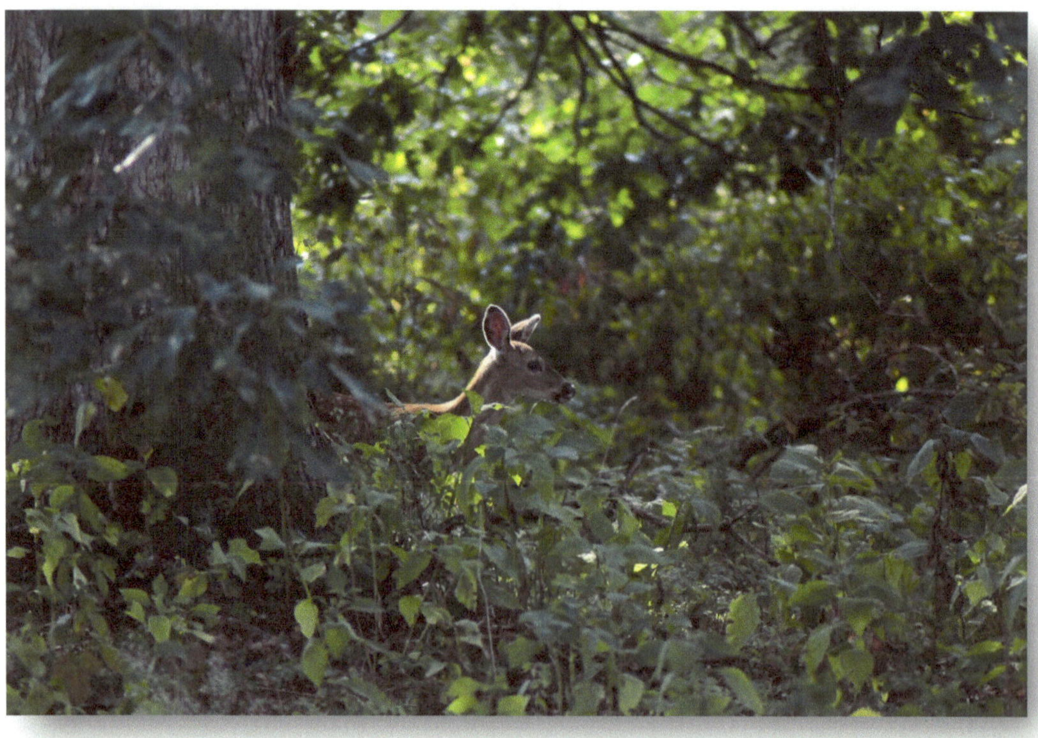

Bugs and Critters

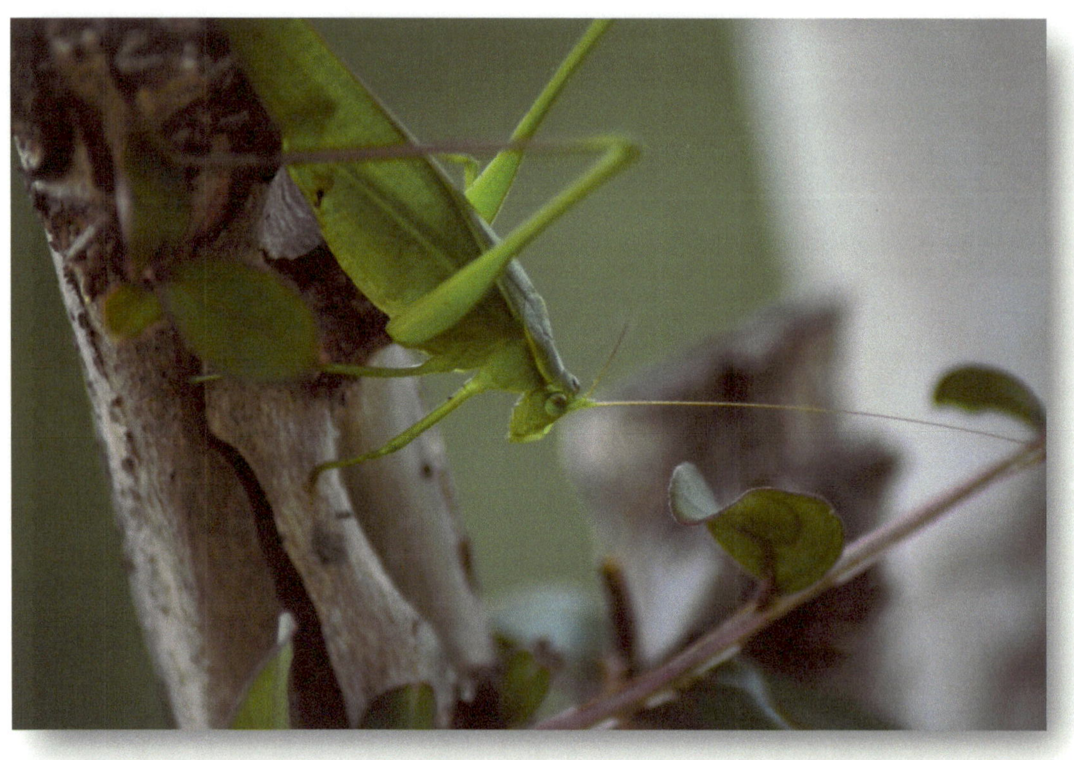

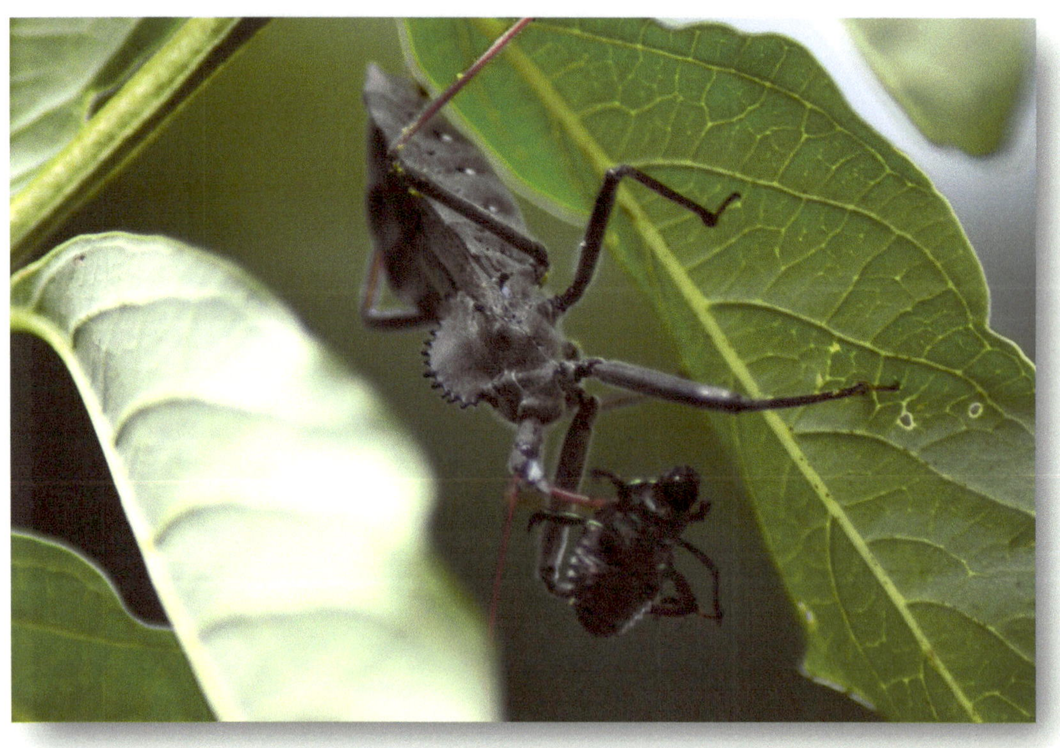

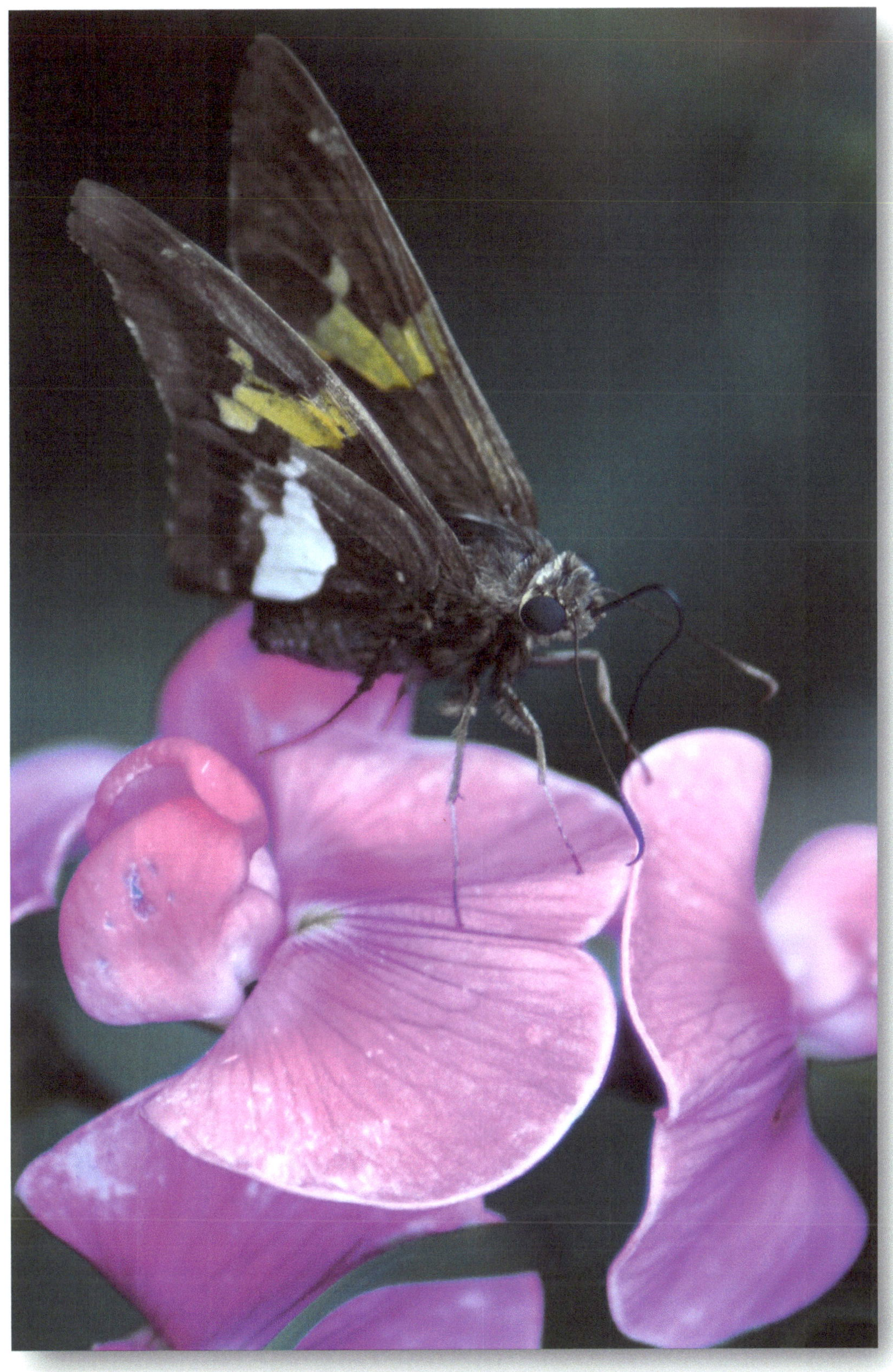

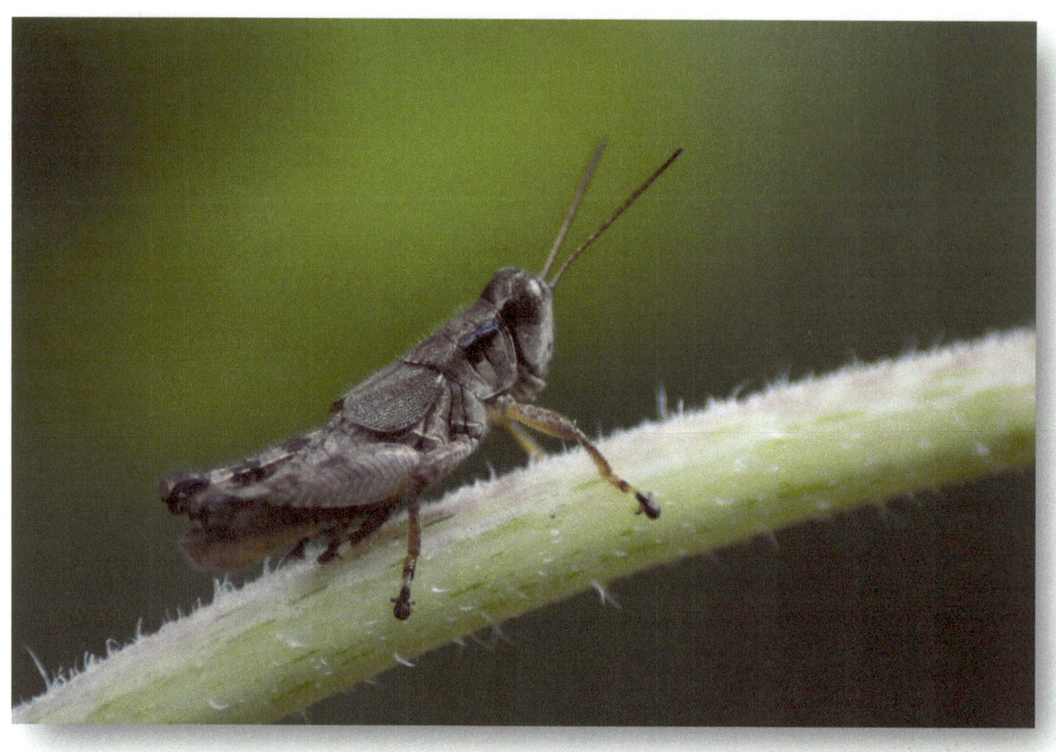

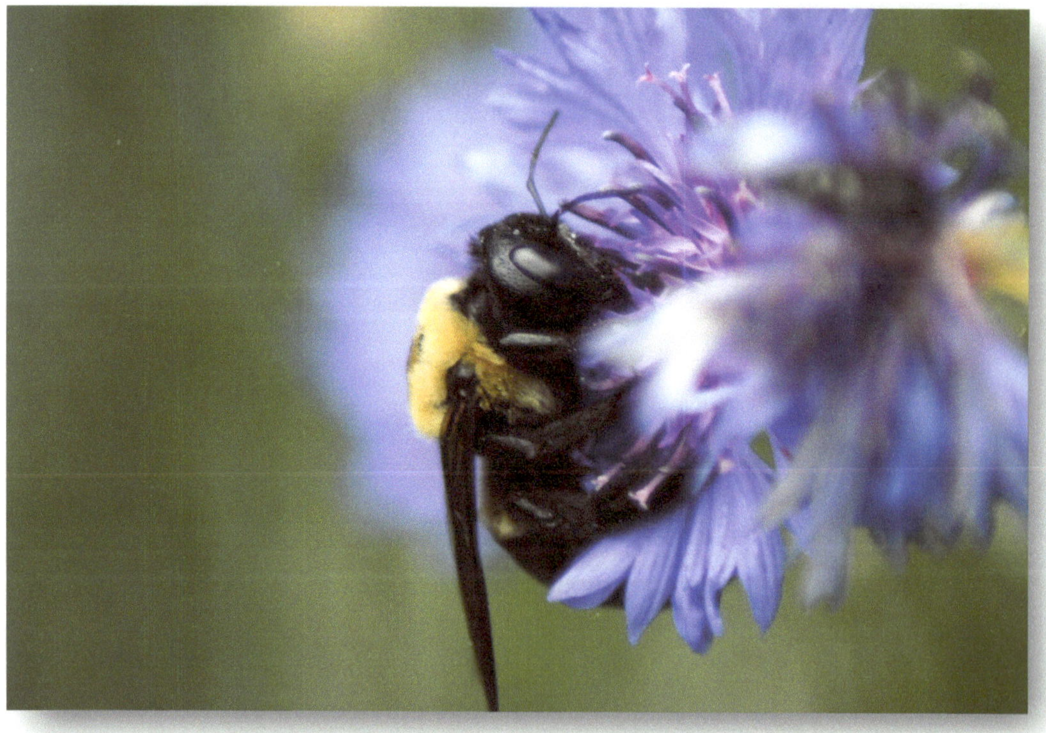

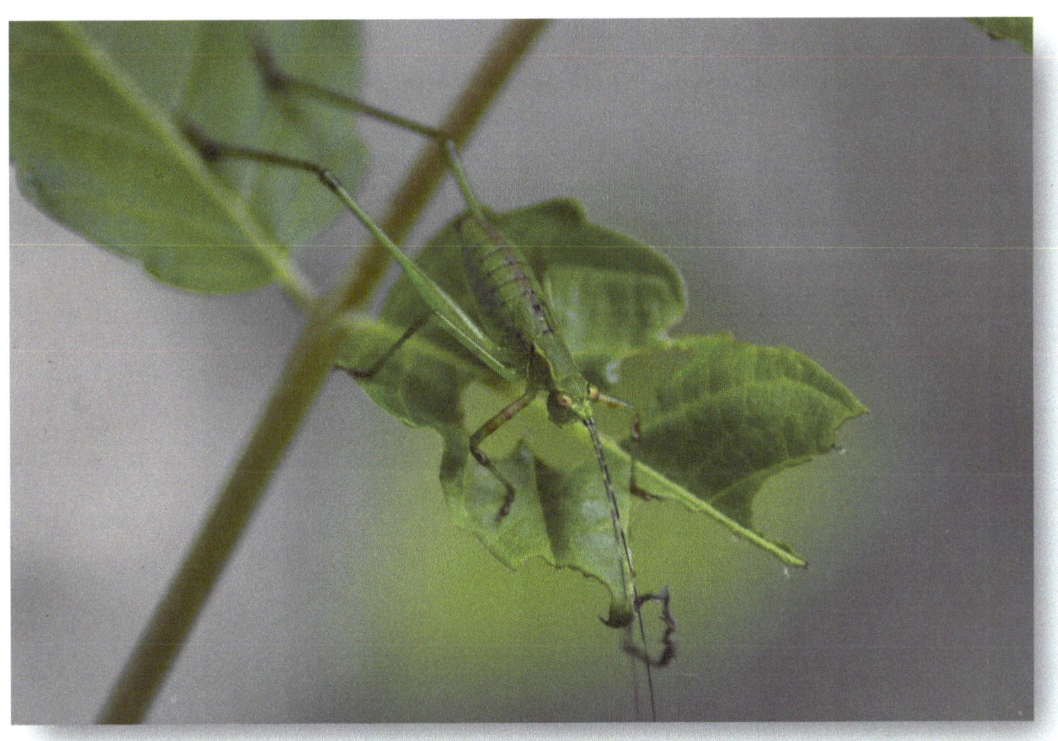

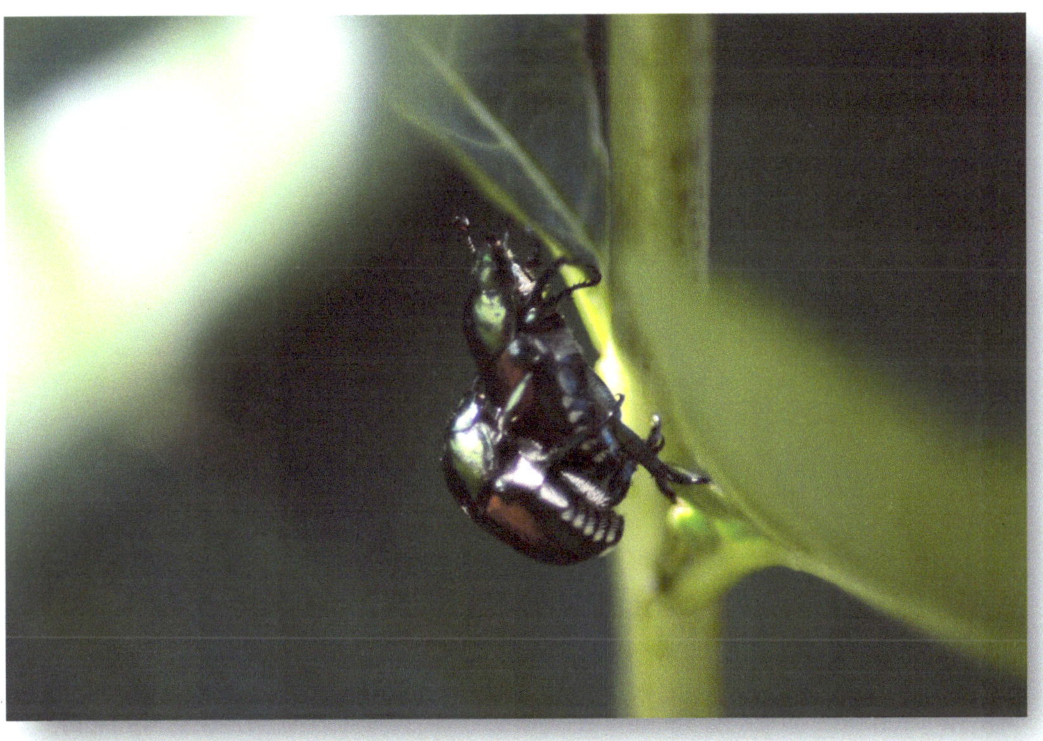

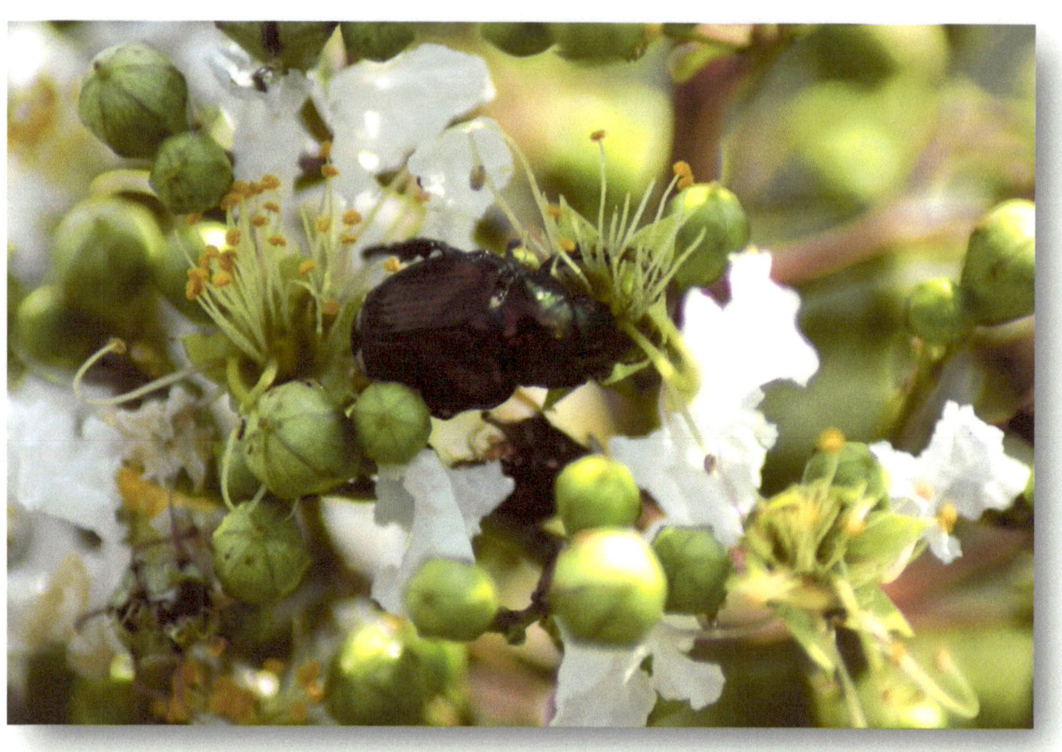

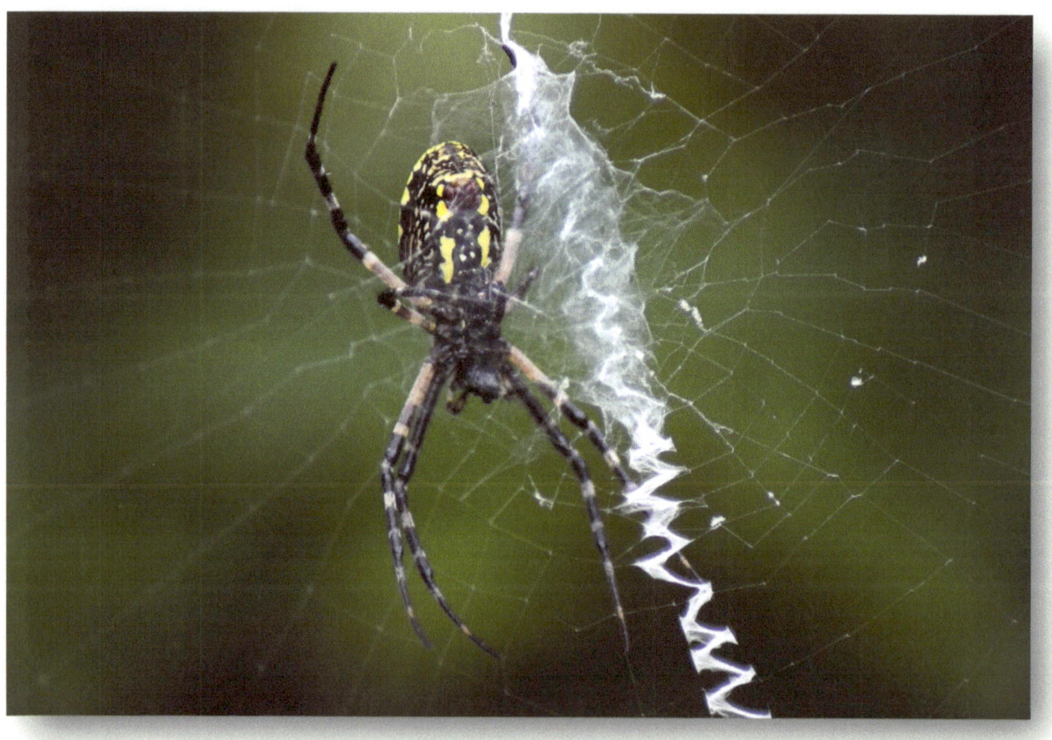

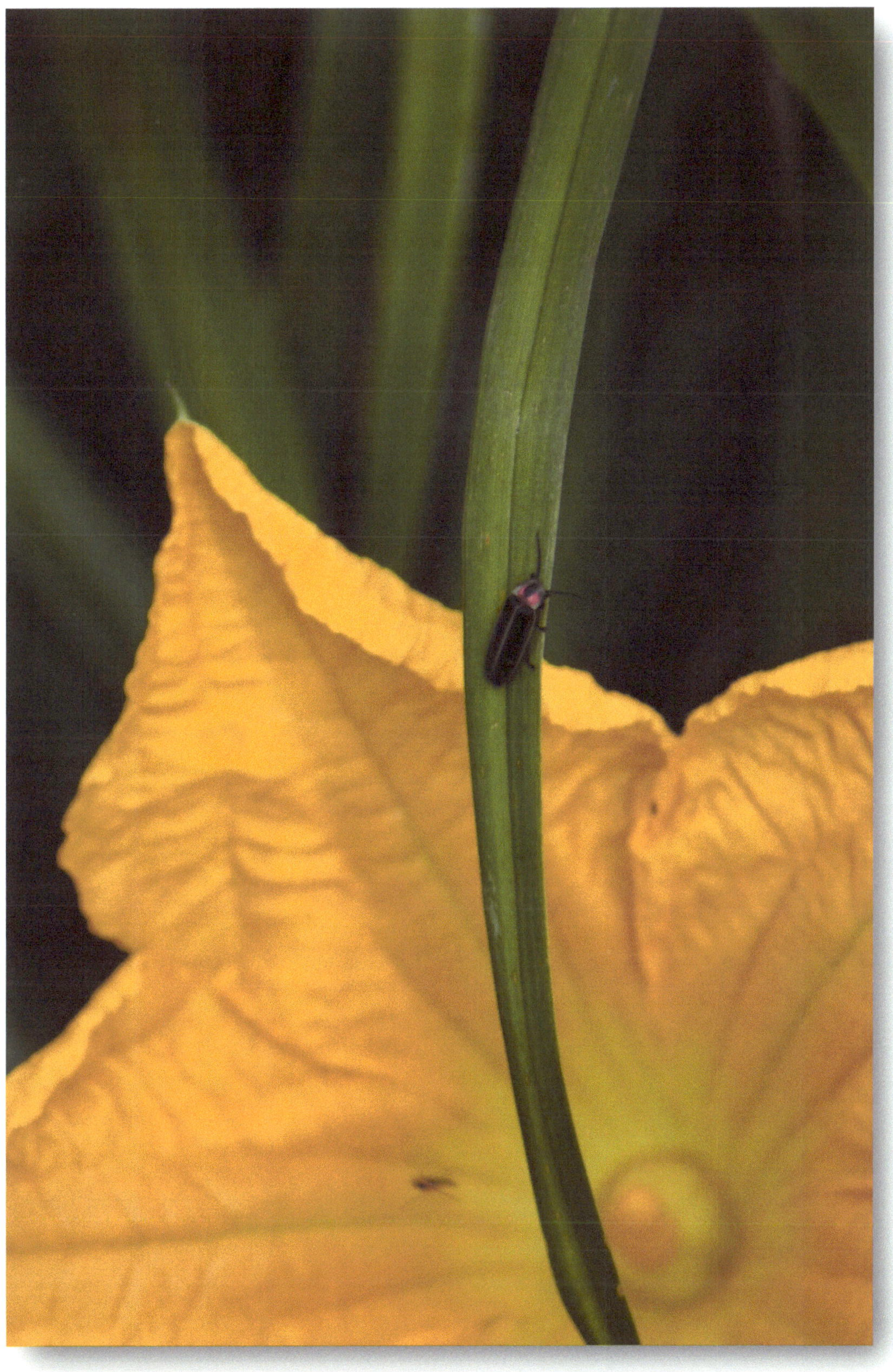

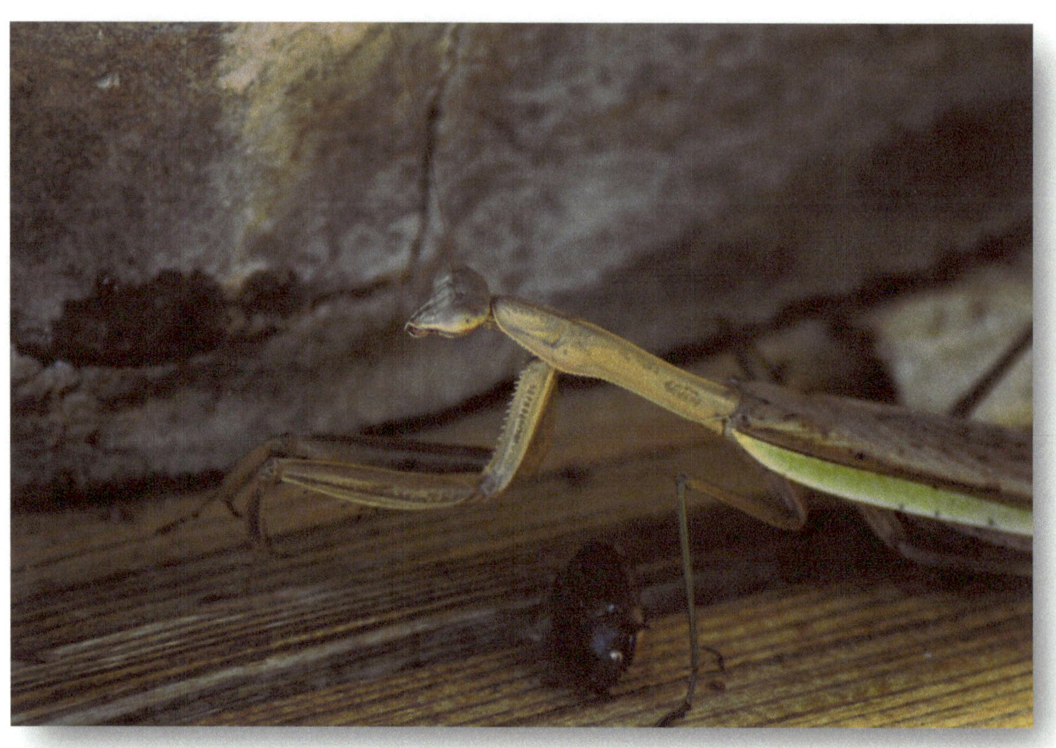

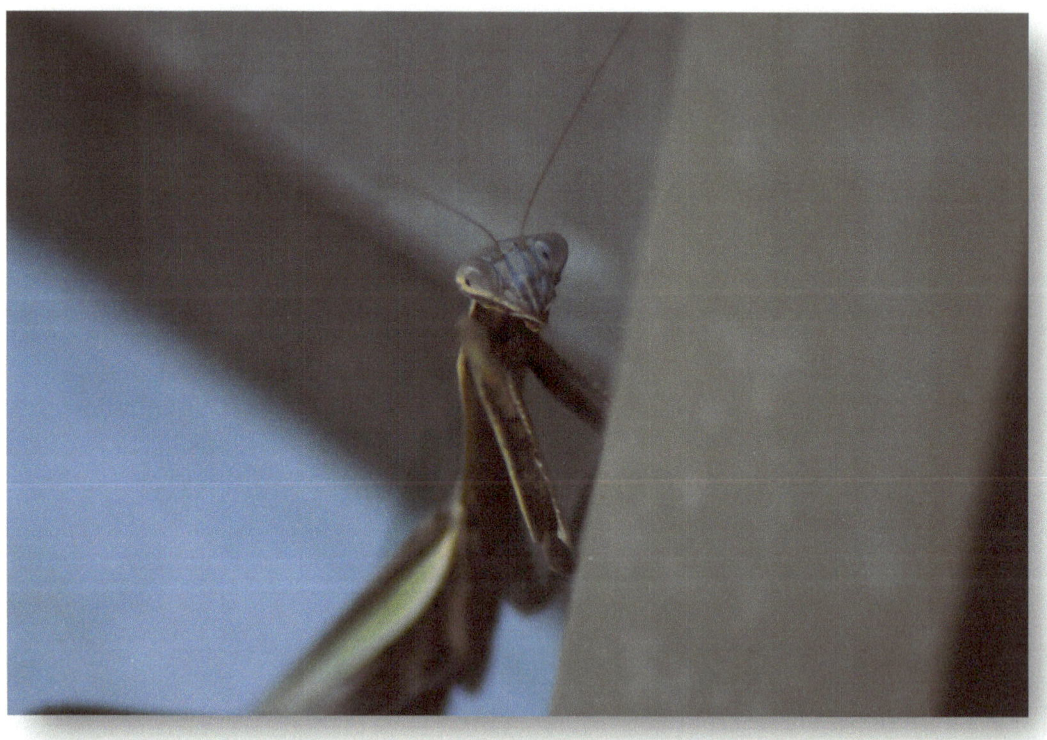

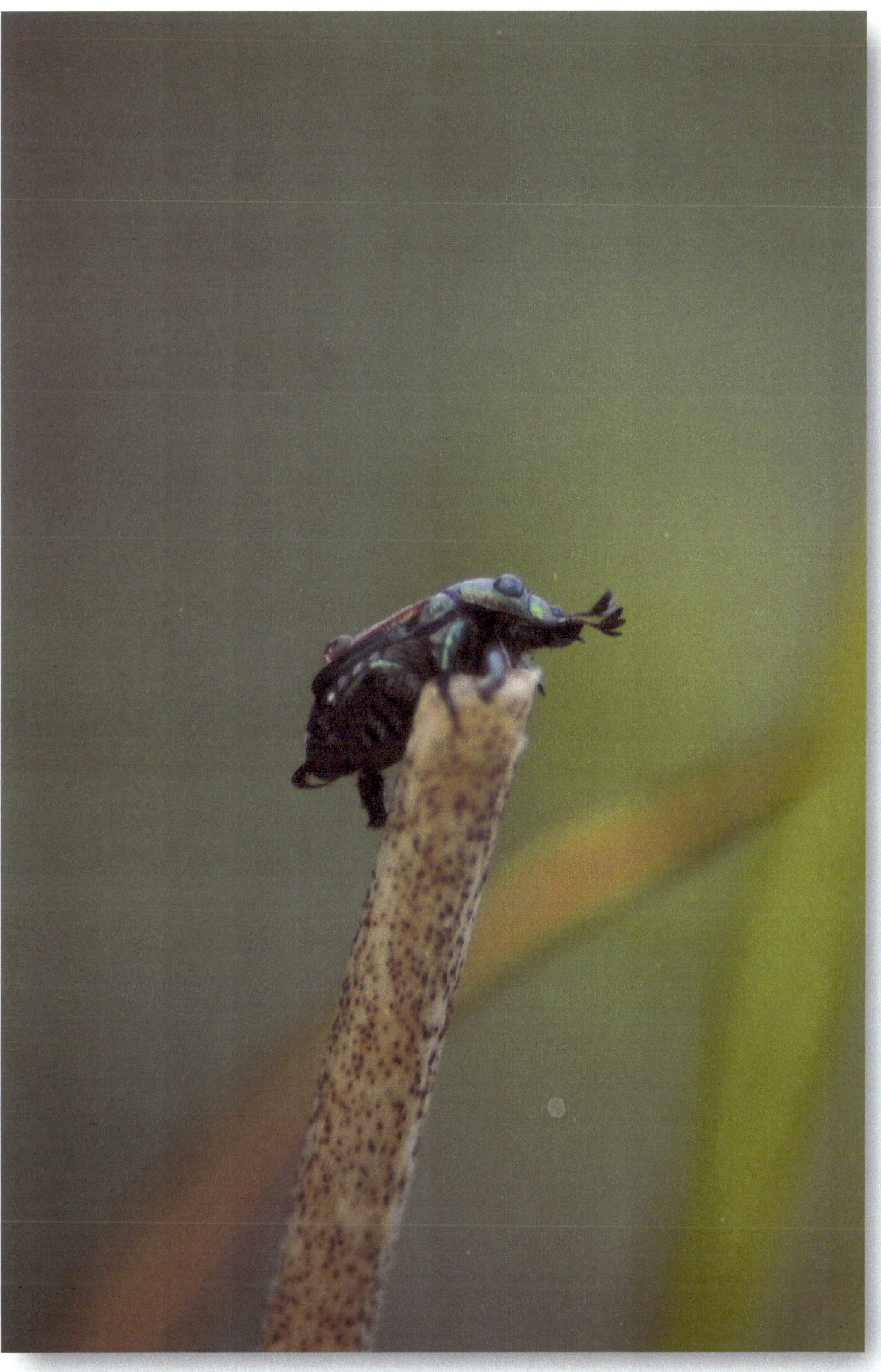

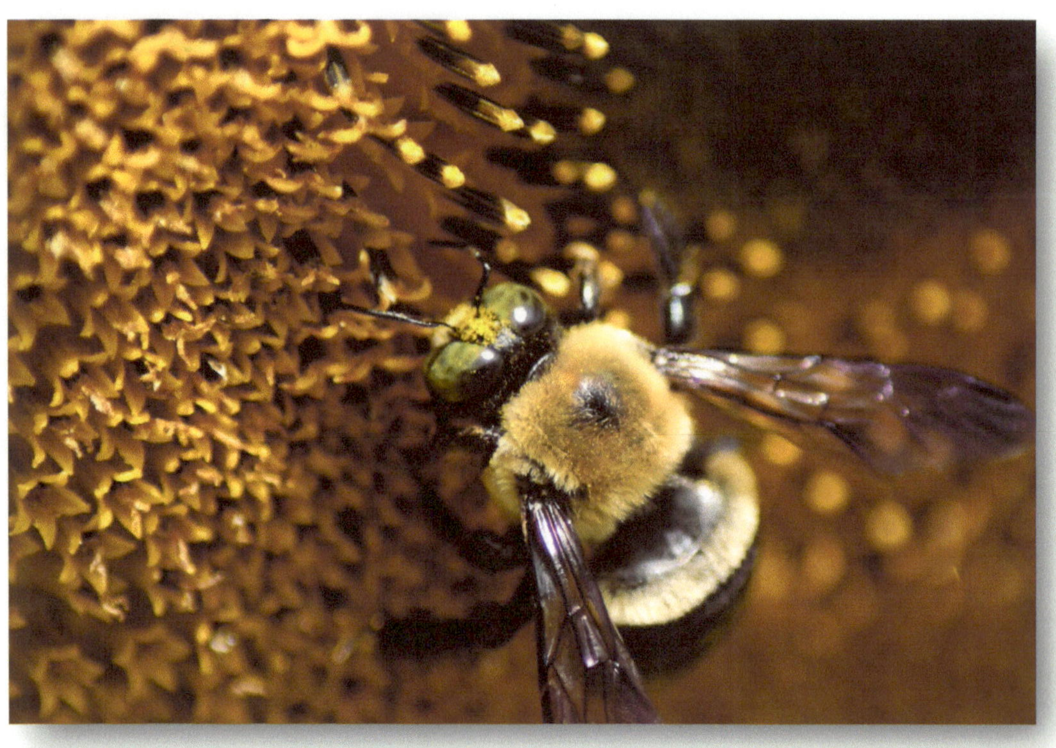

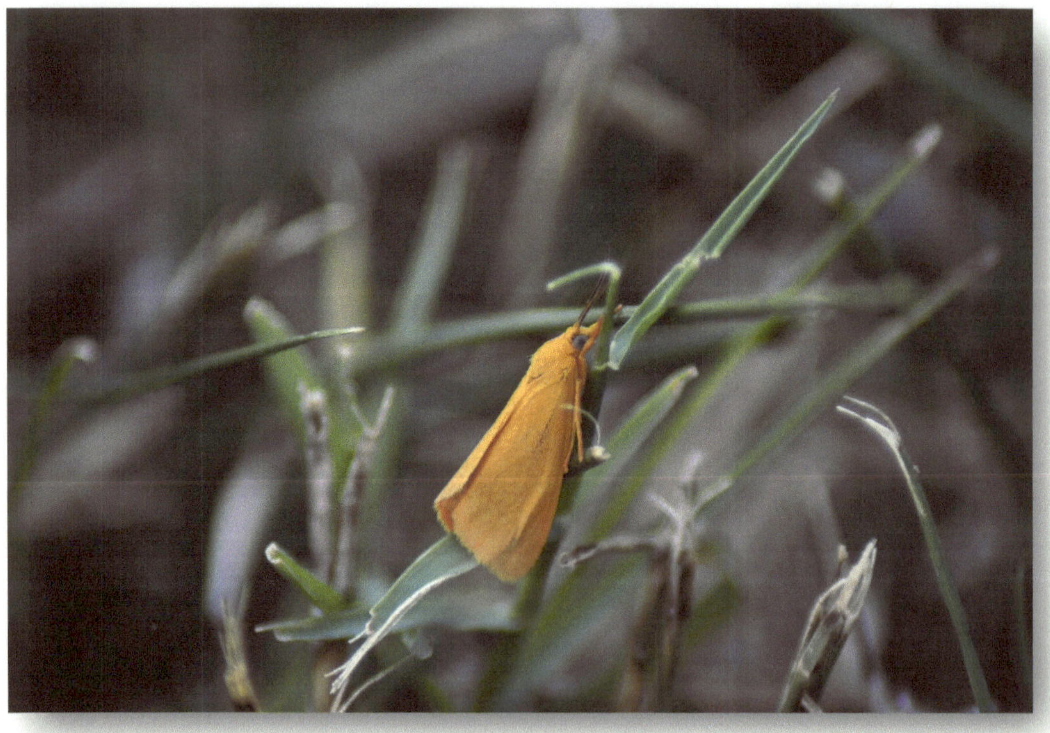

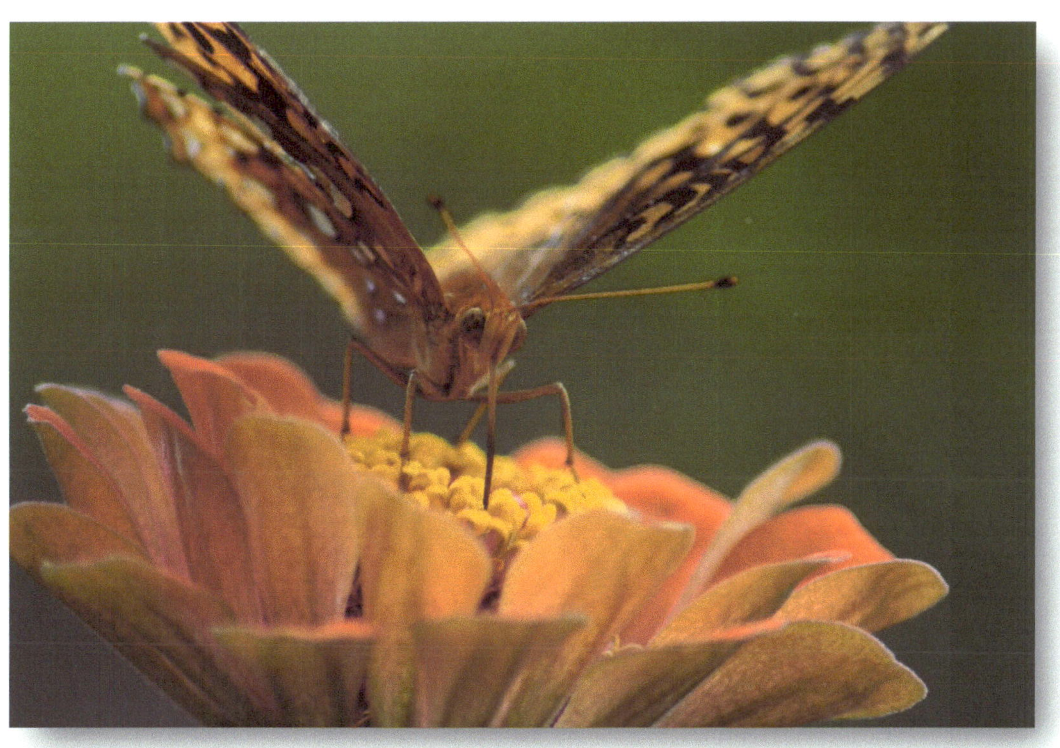

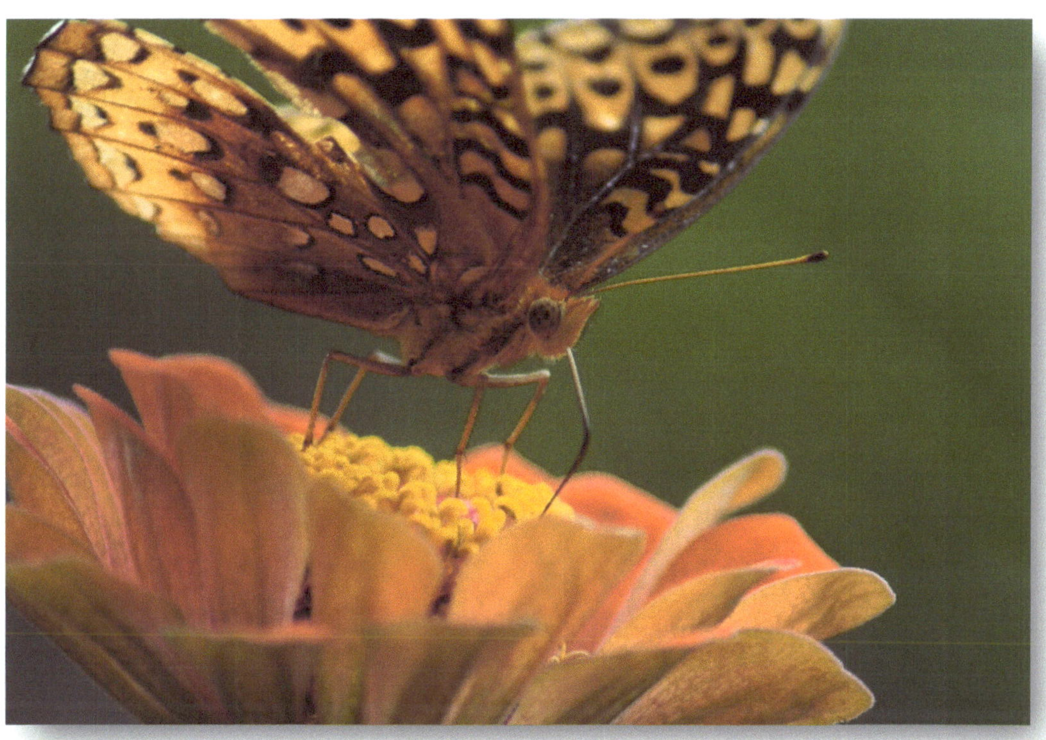

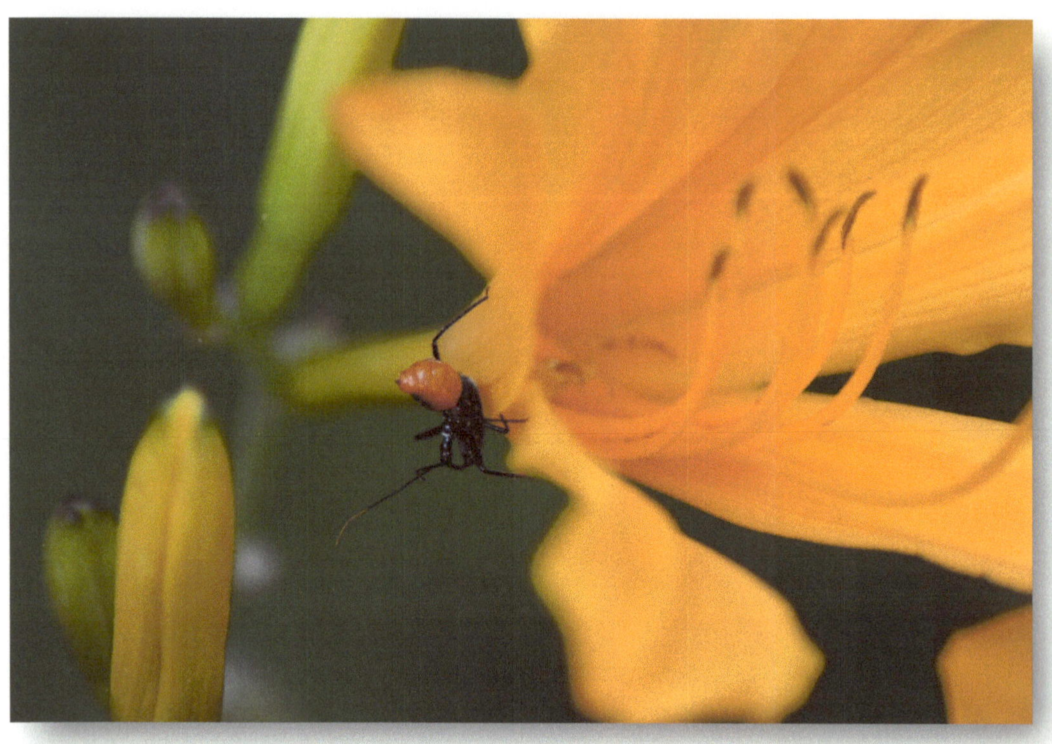

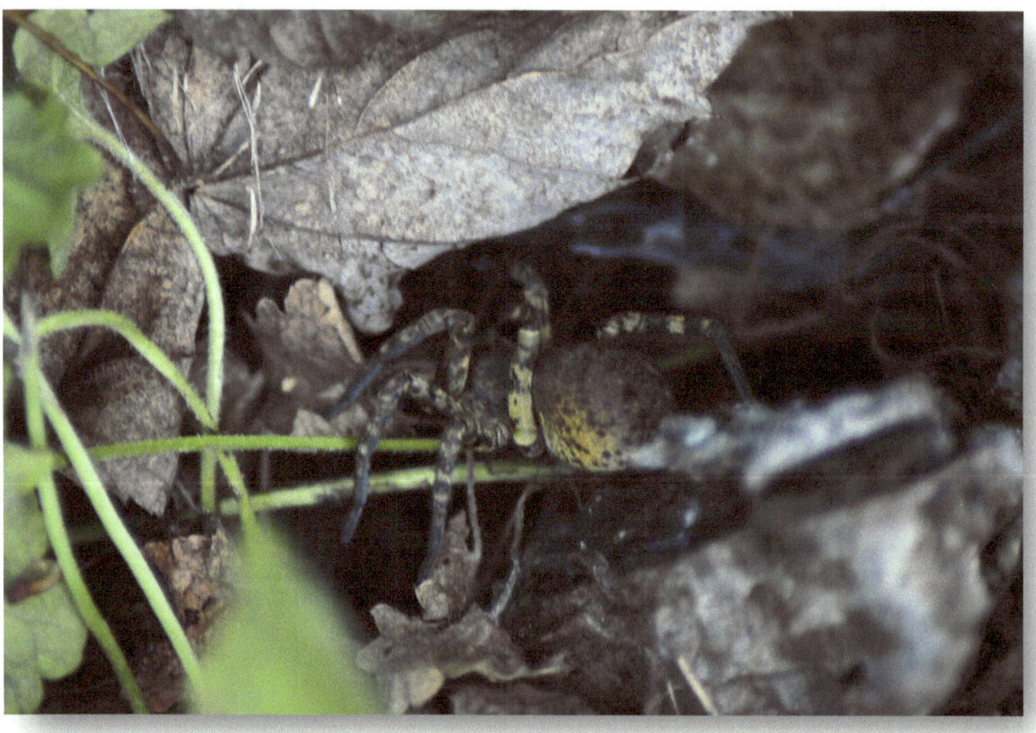

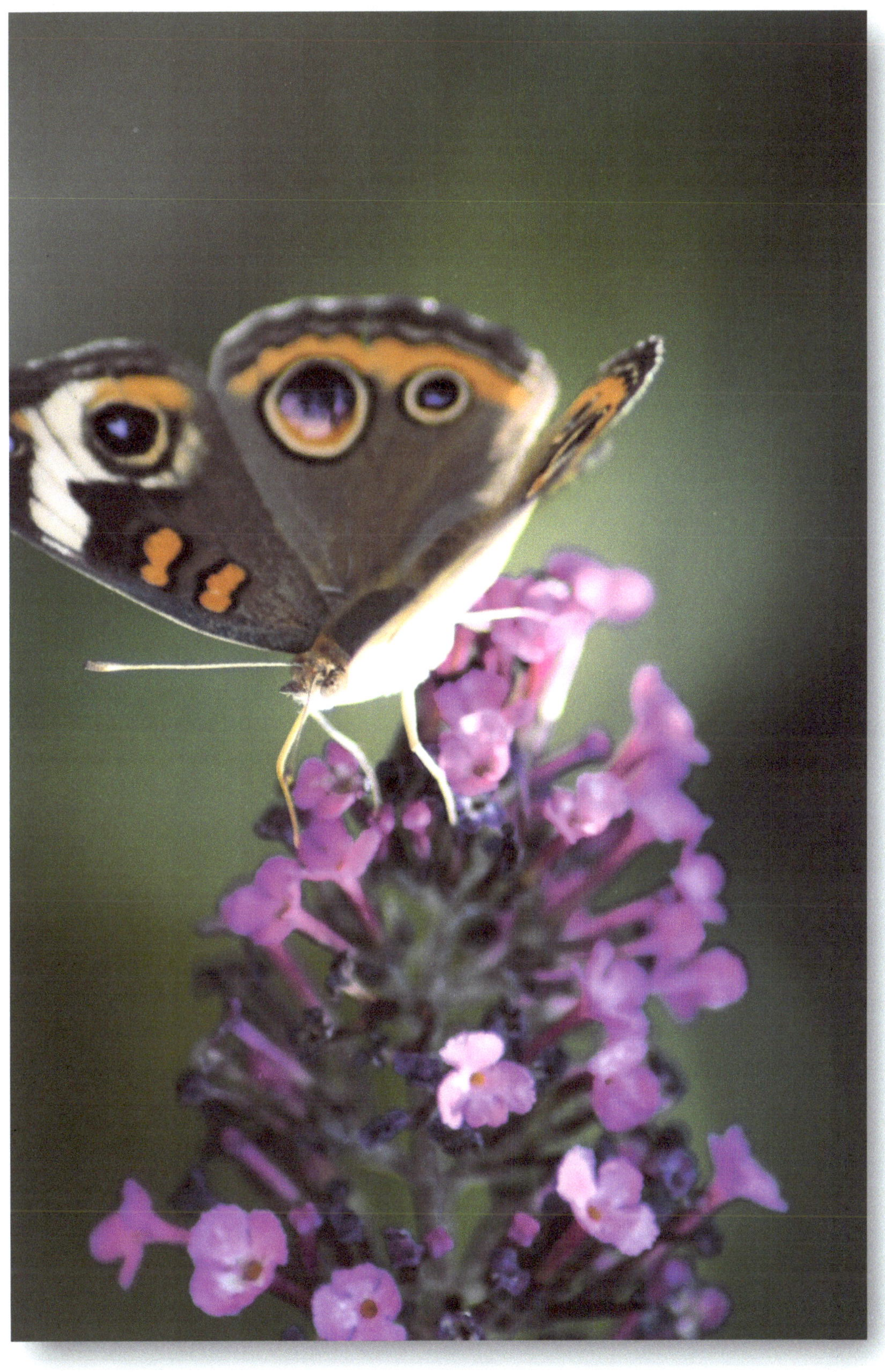

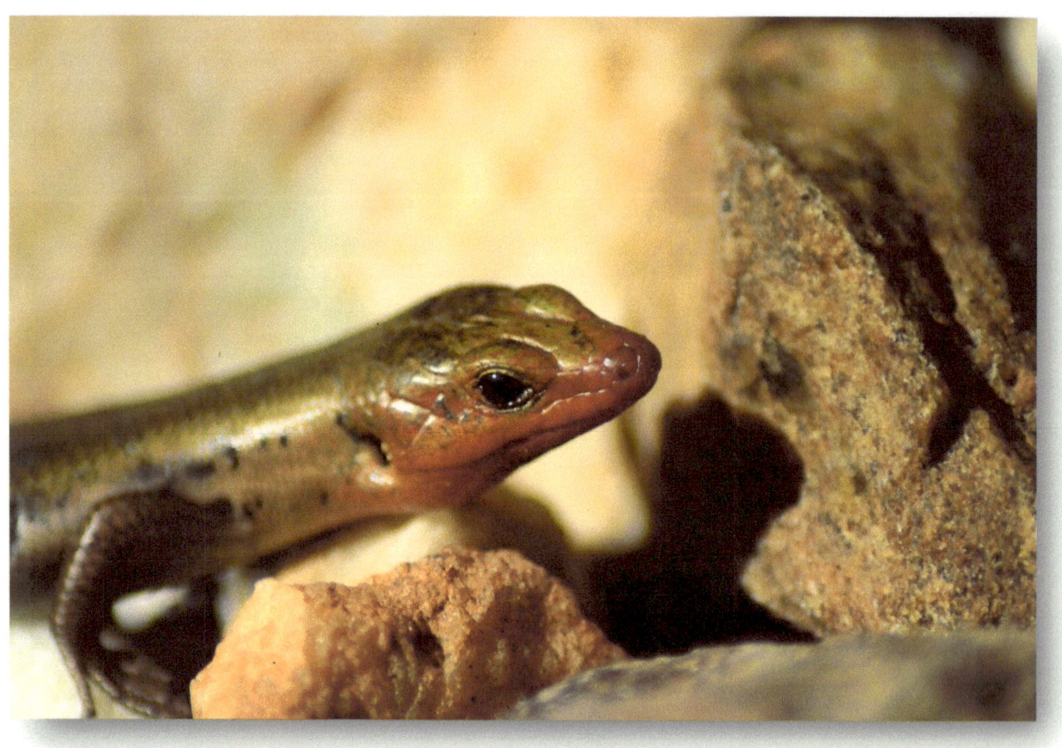

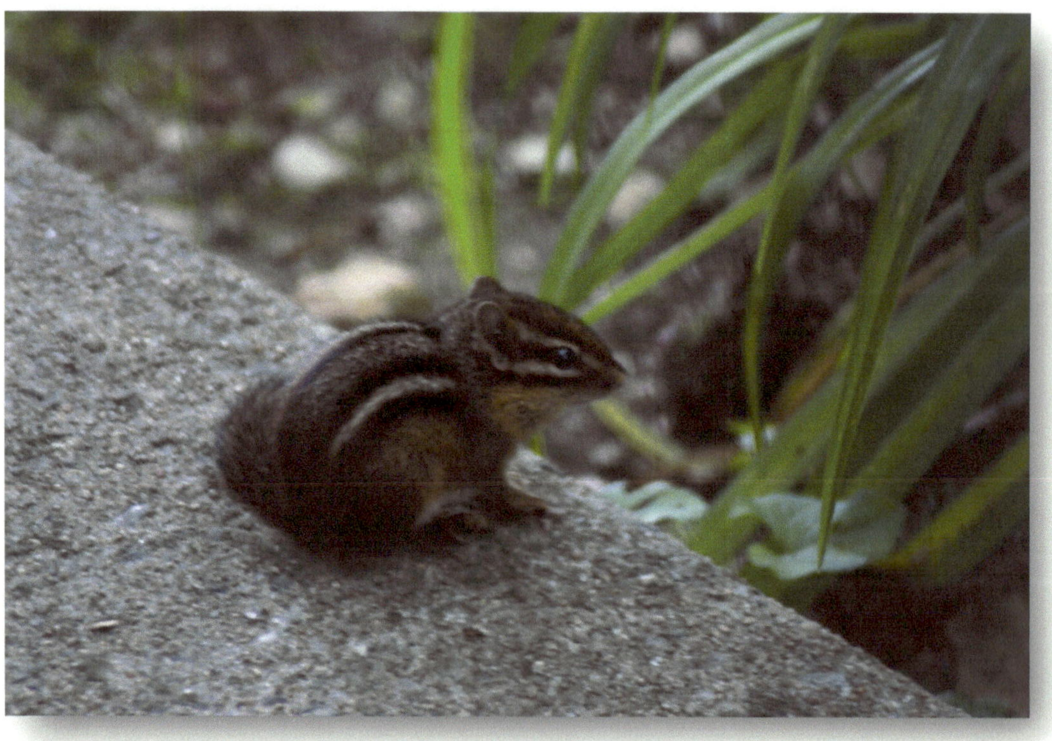

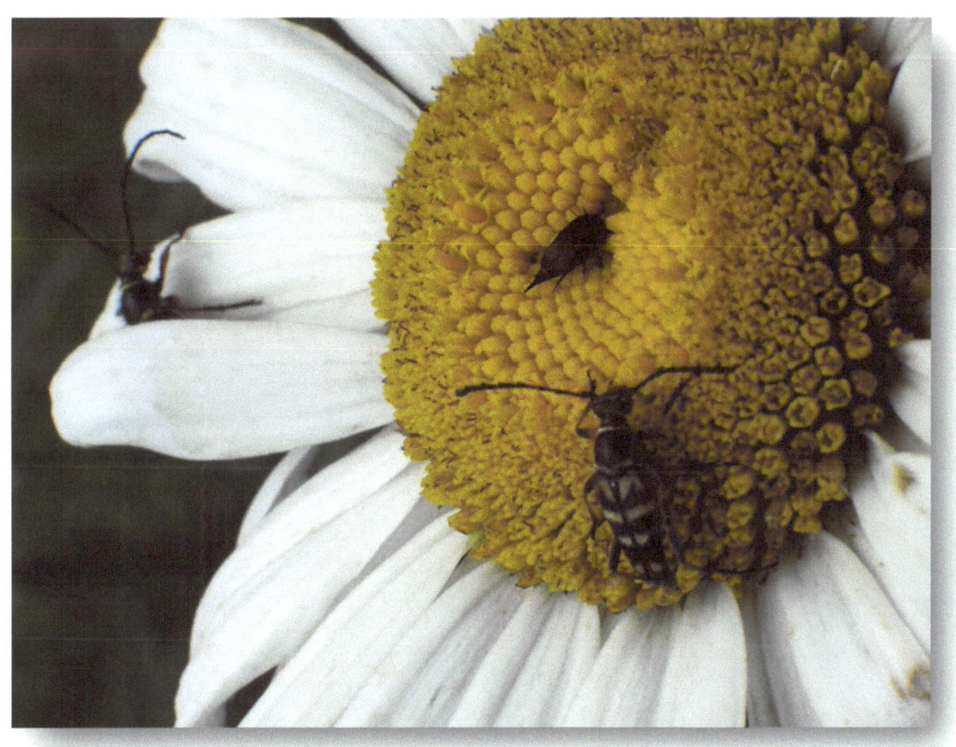

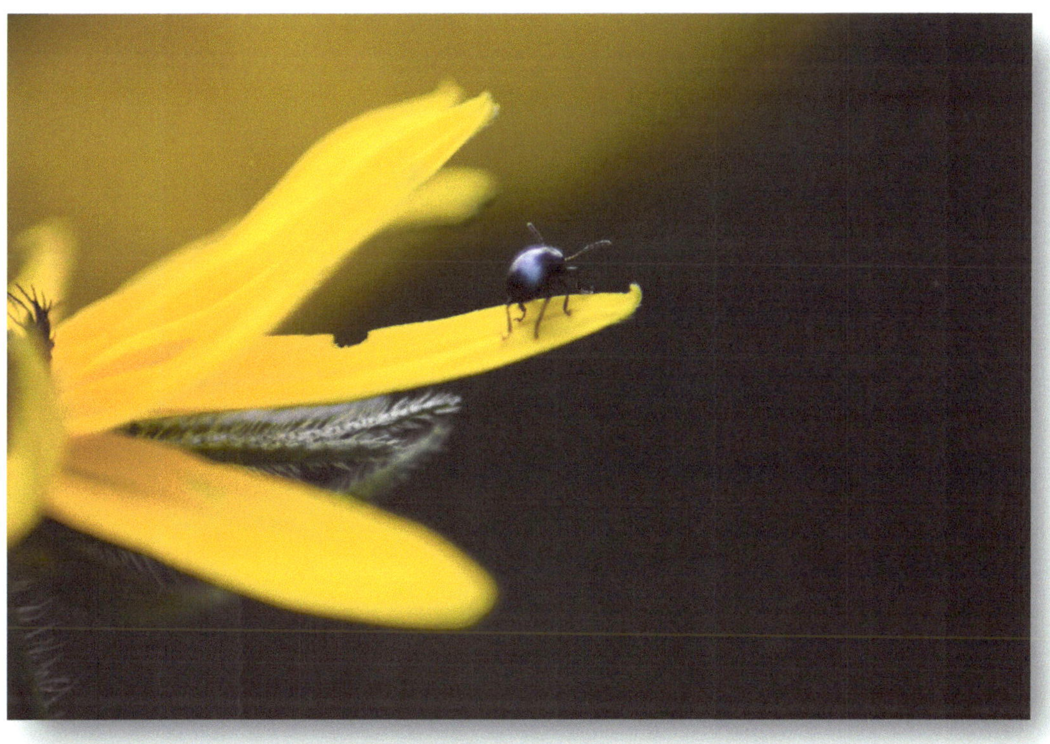

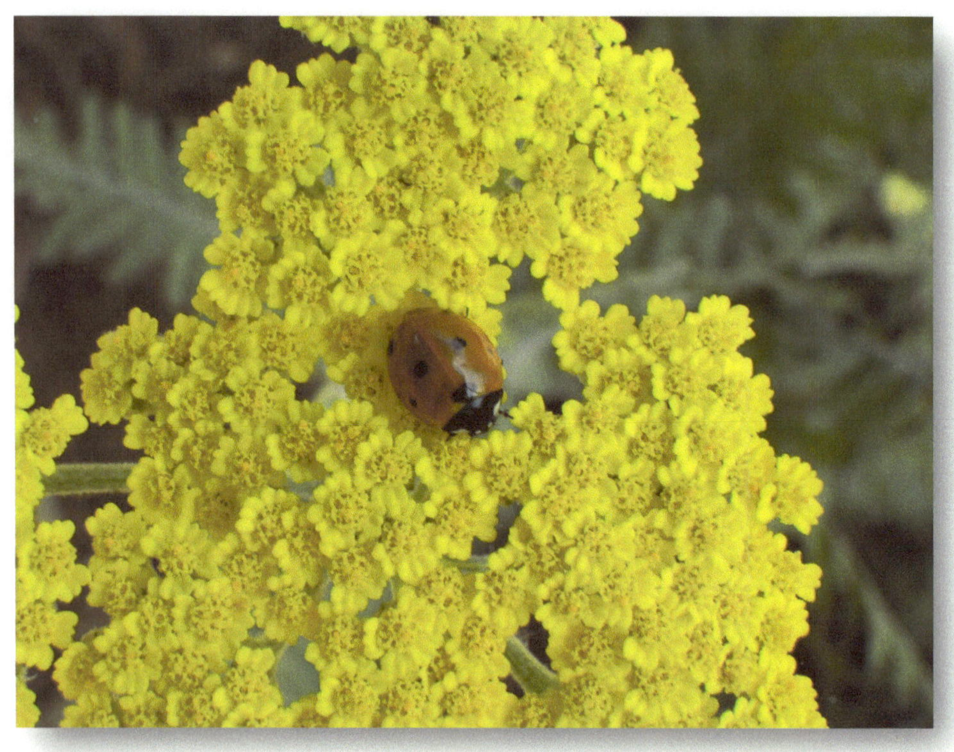

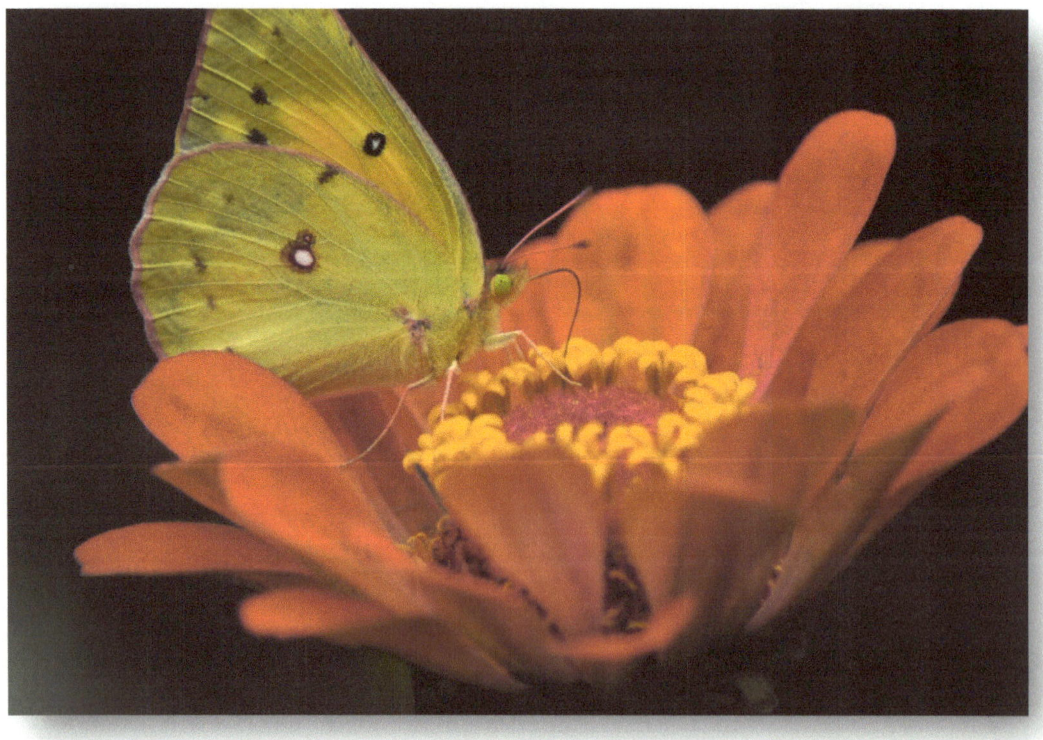

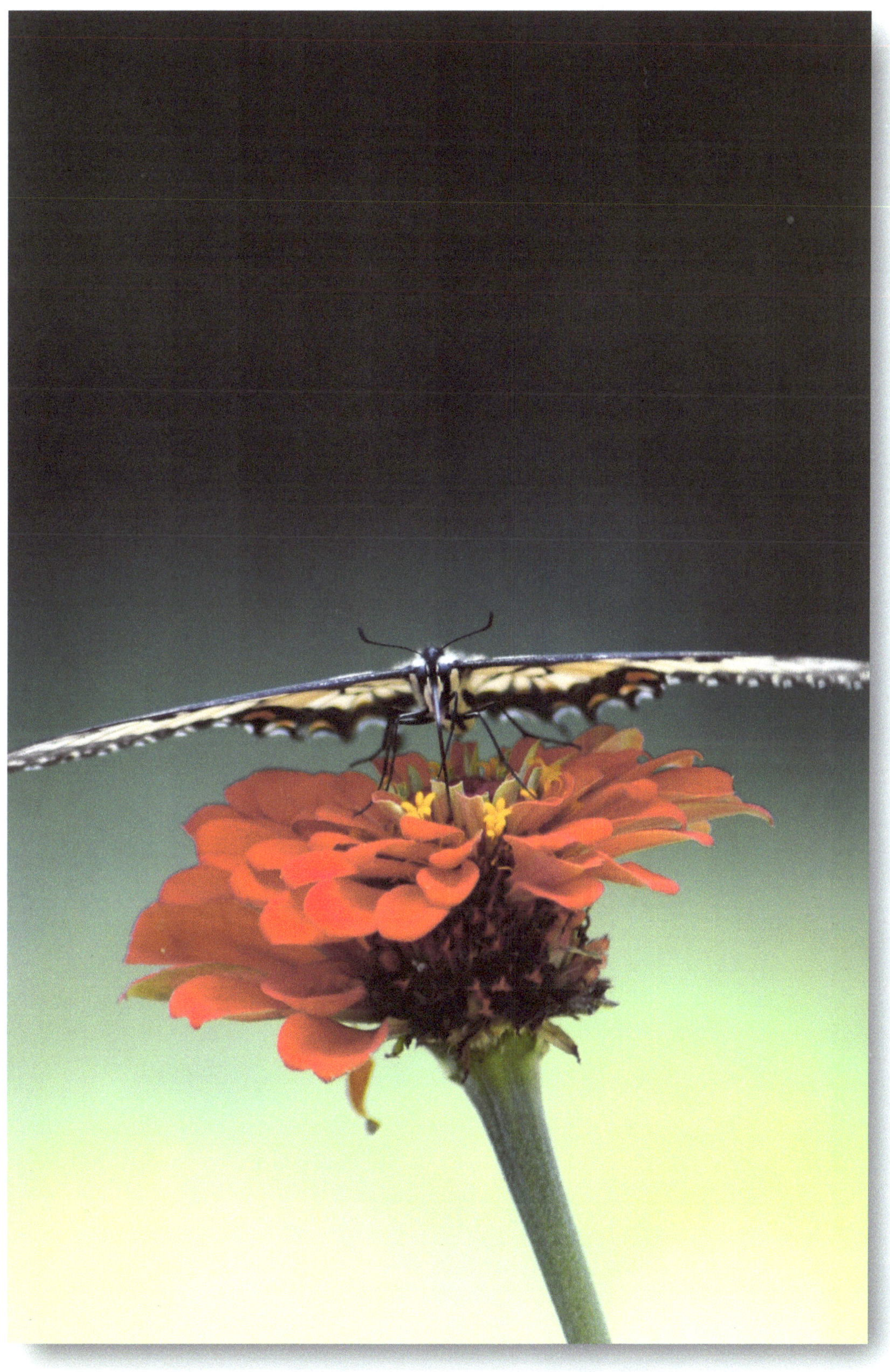

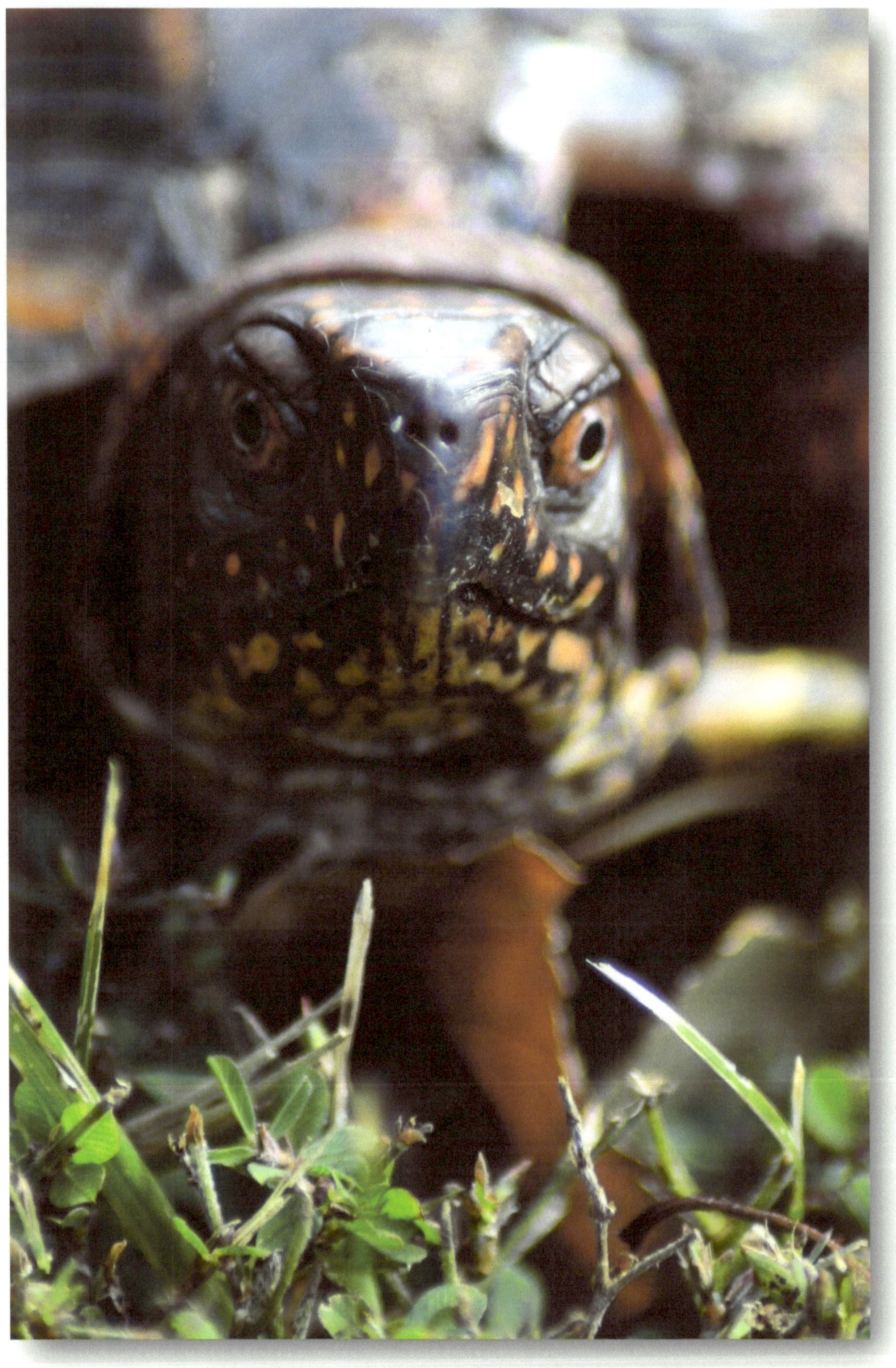

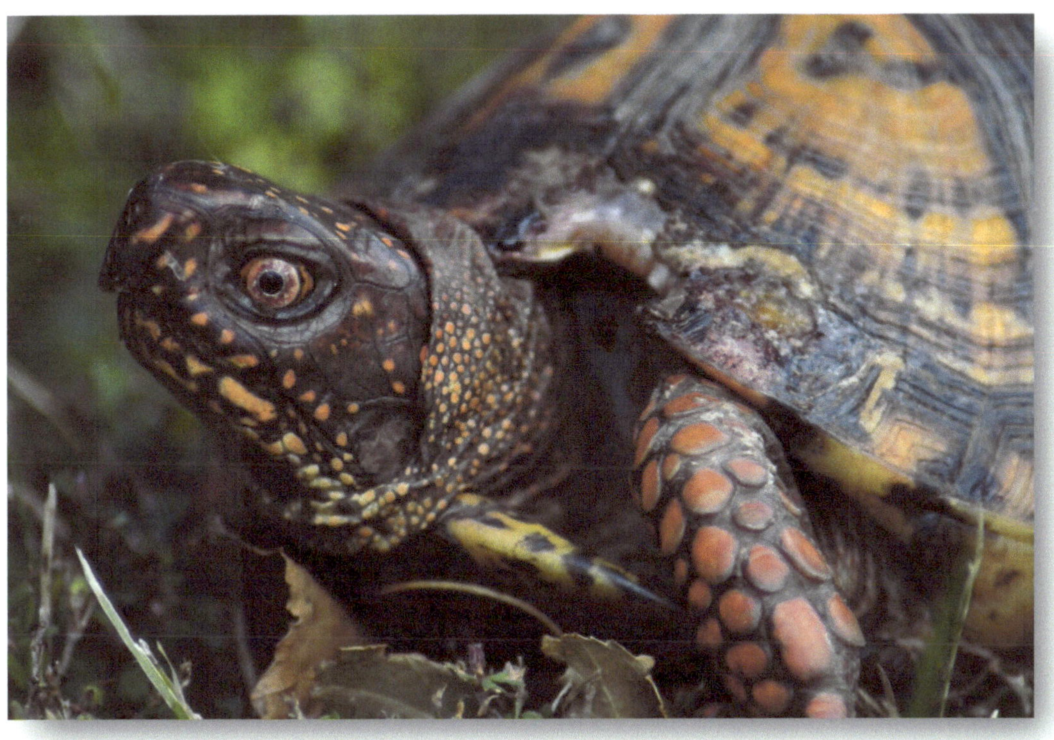

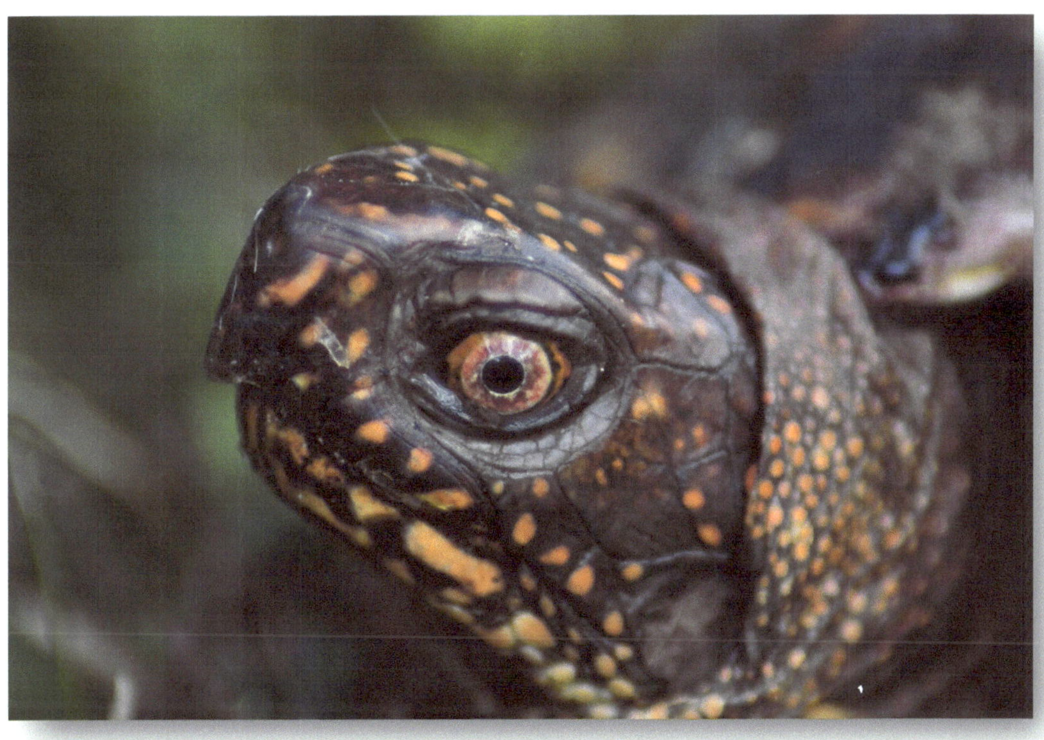

Birds

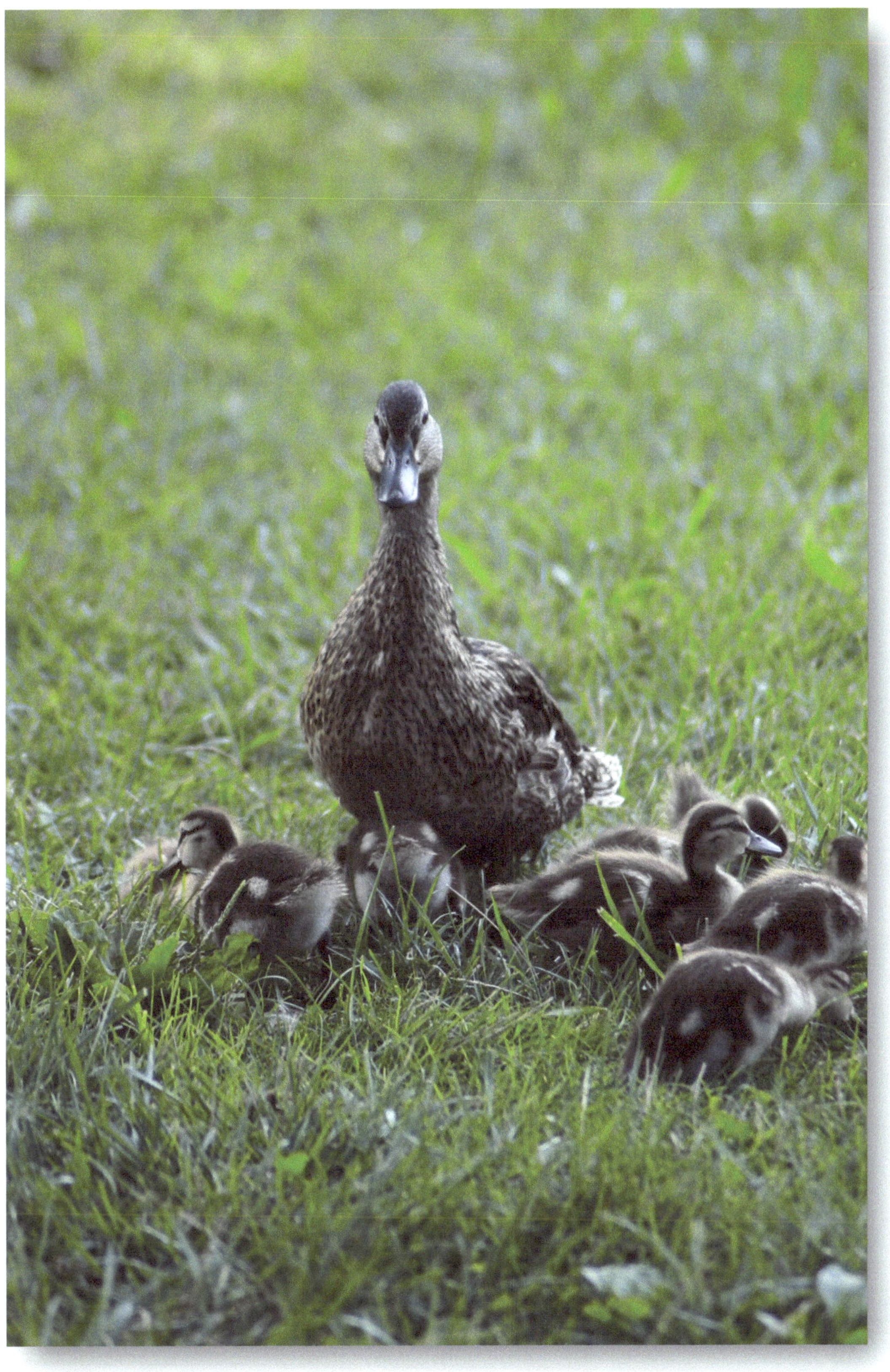

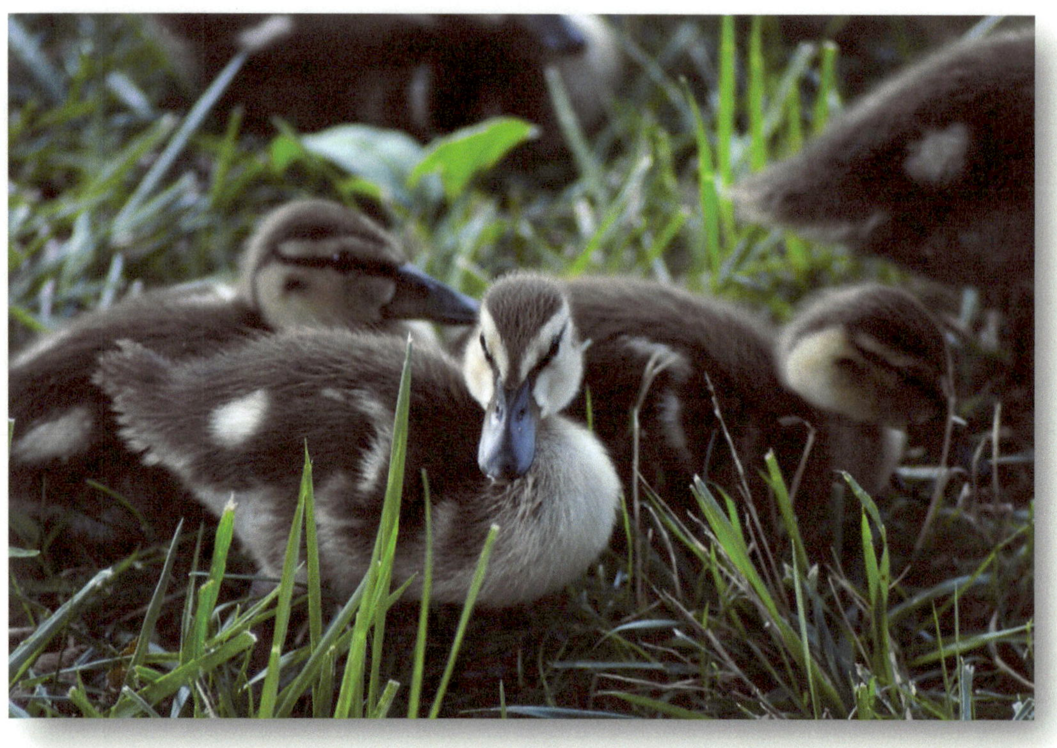

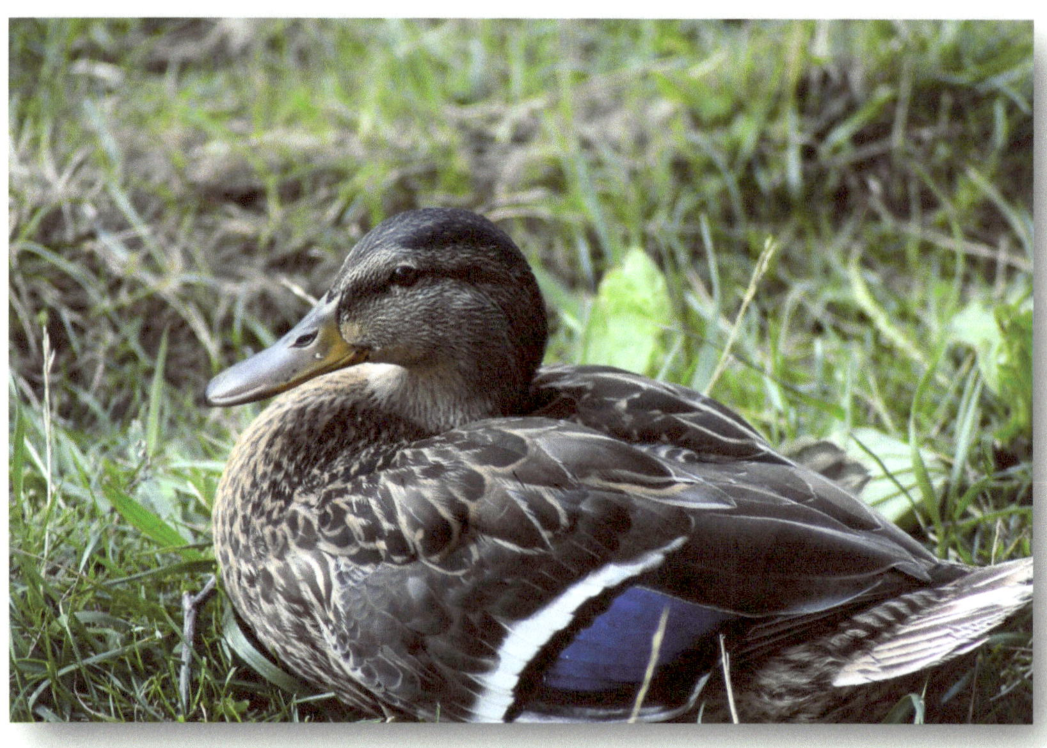

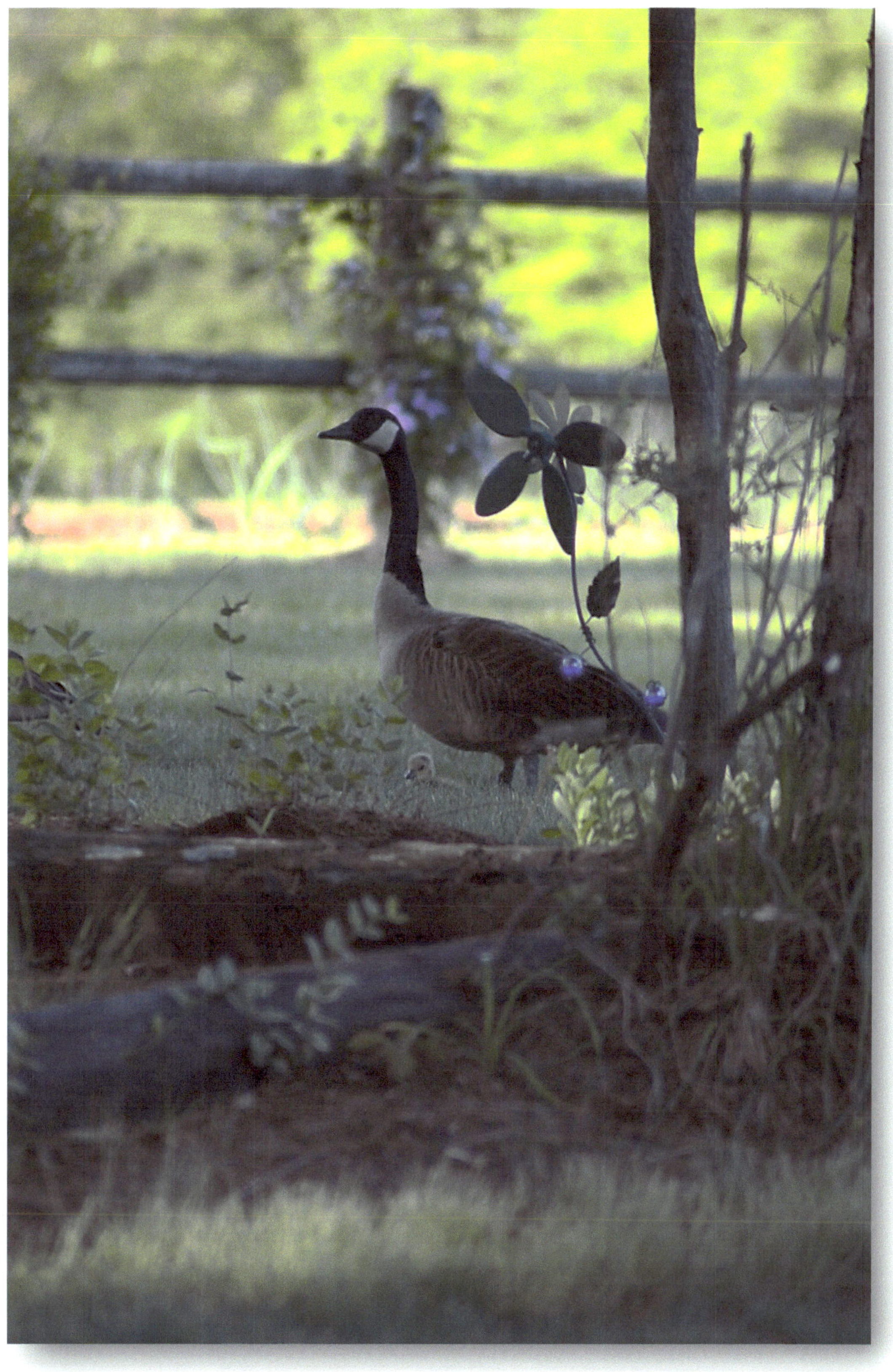

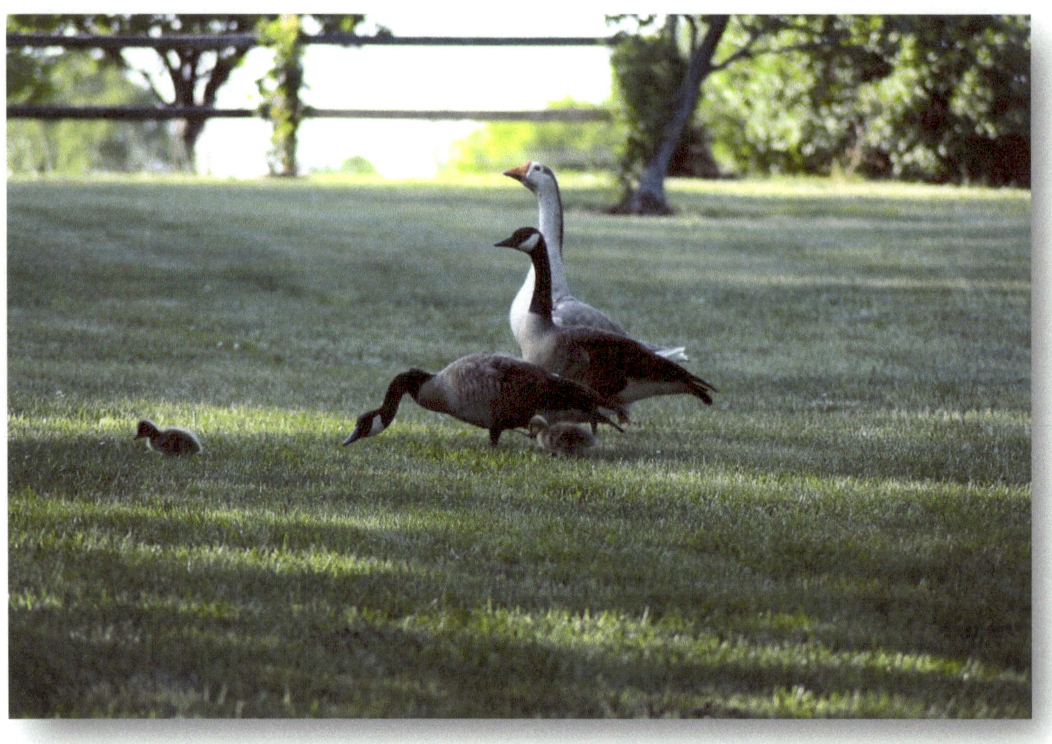

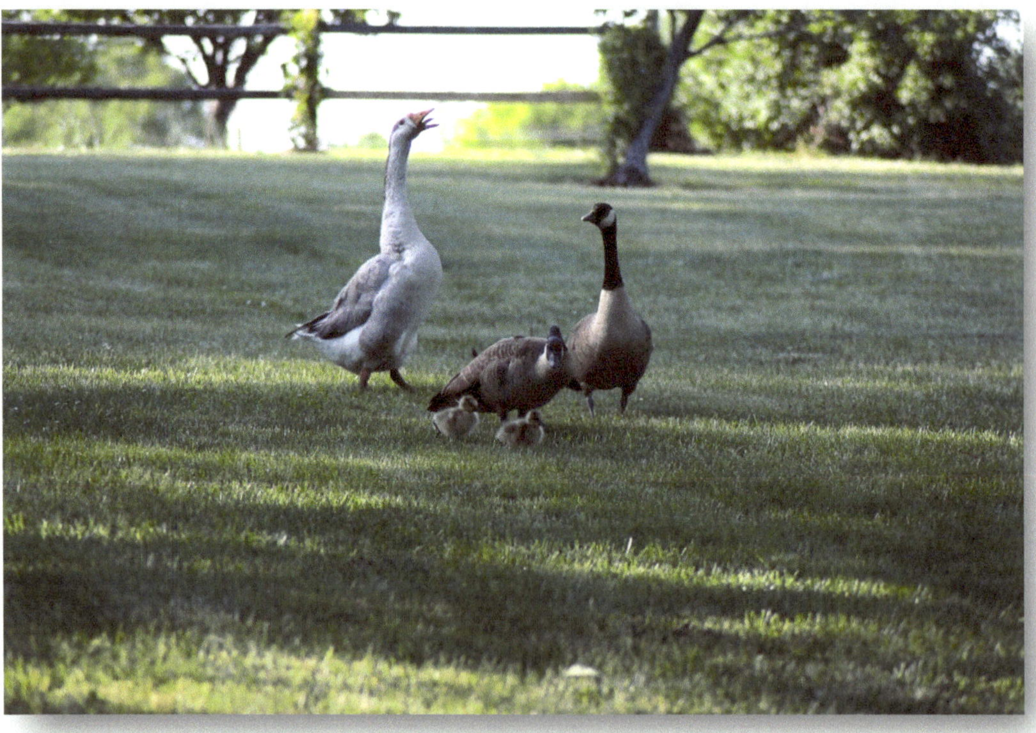

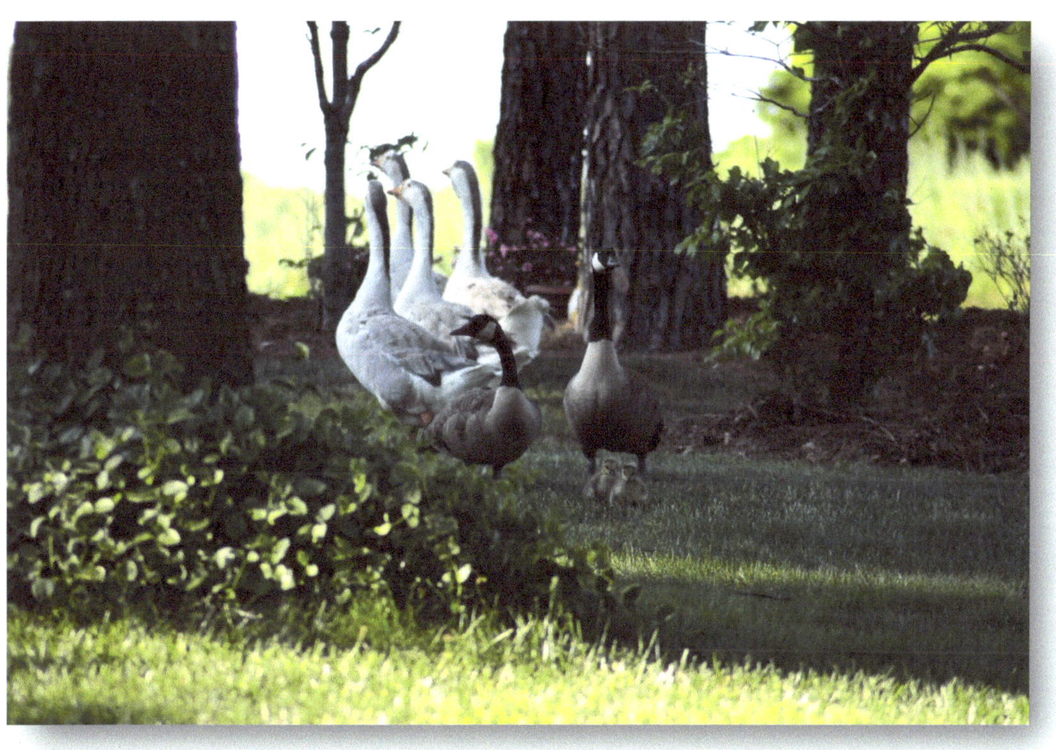

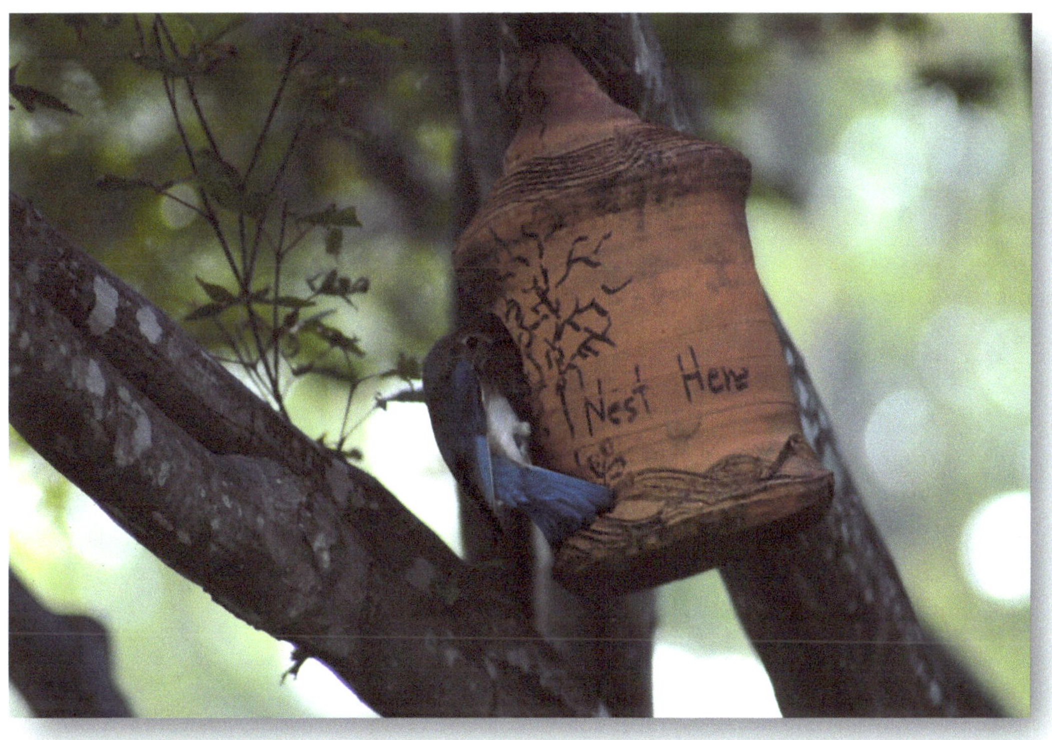
Nest Here

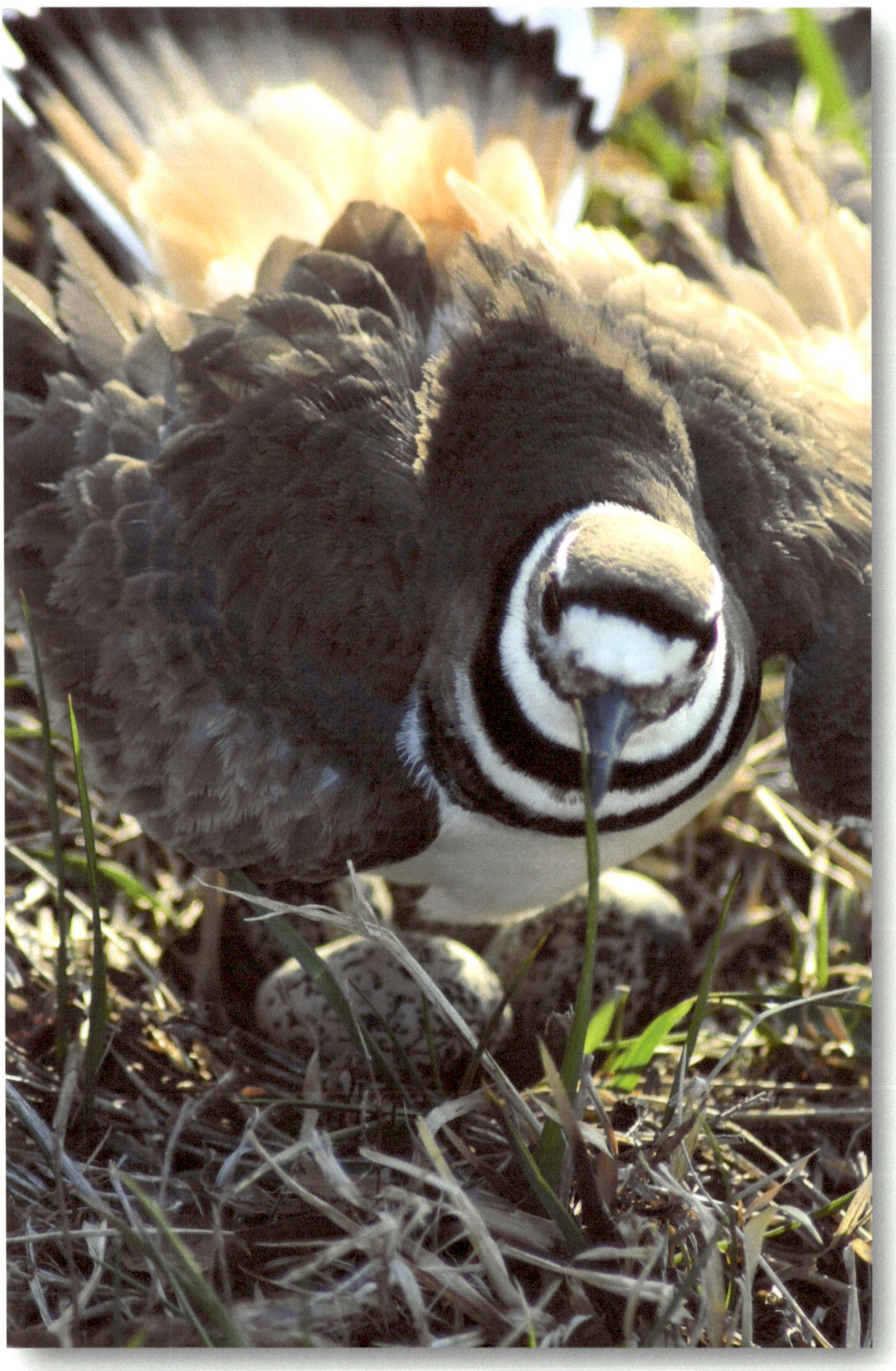

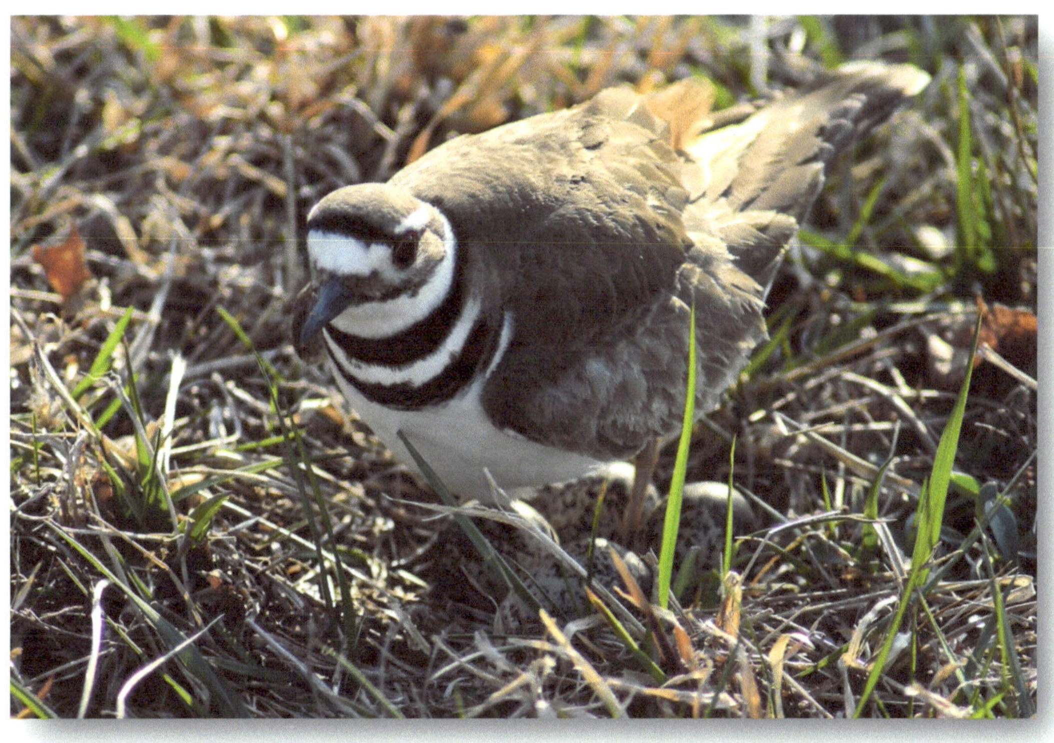

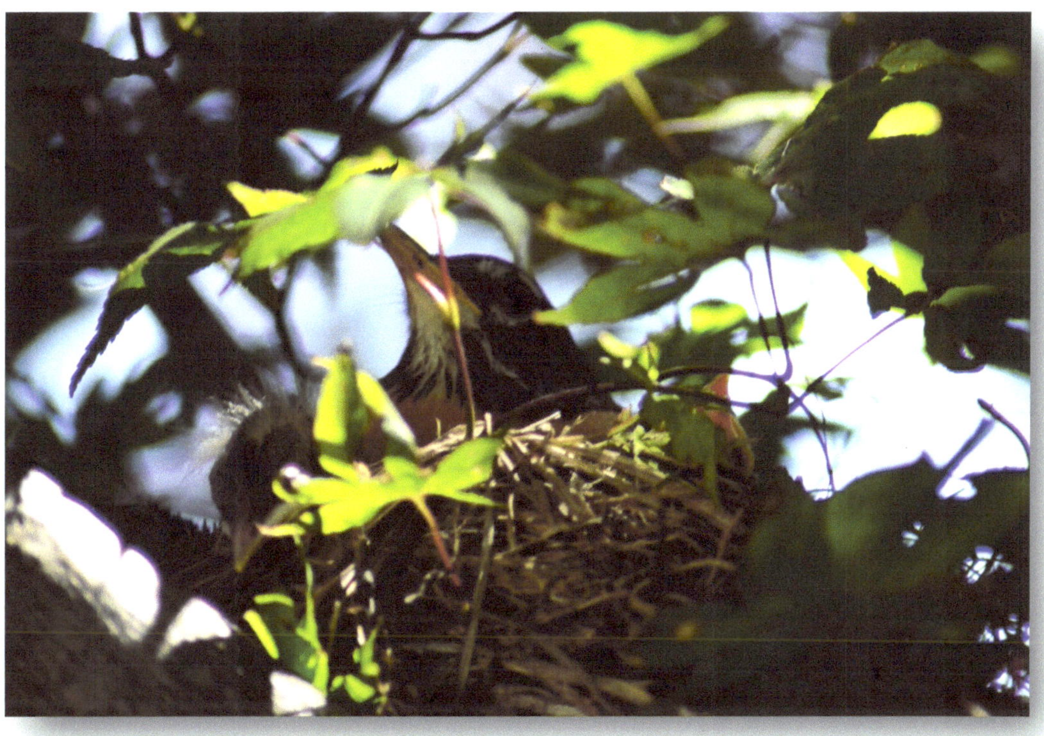

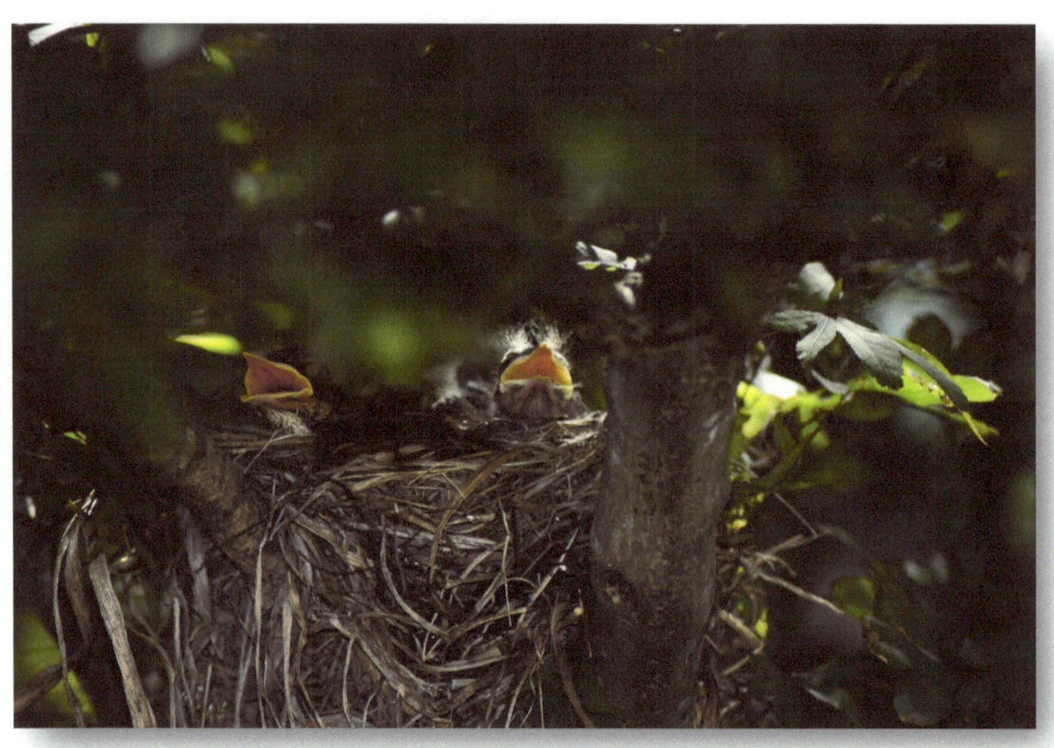

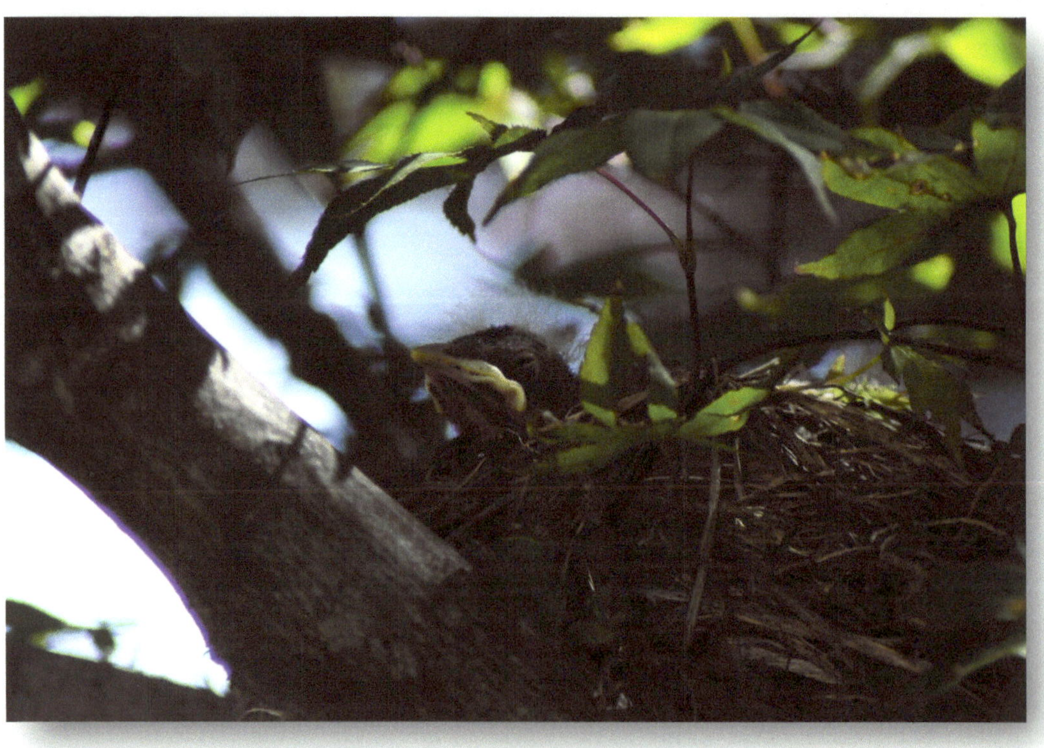

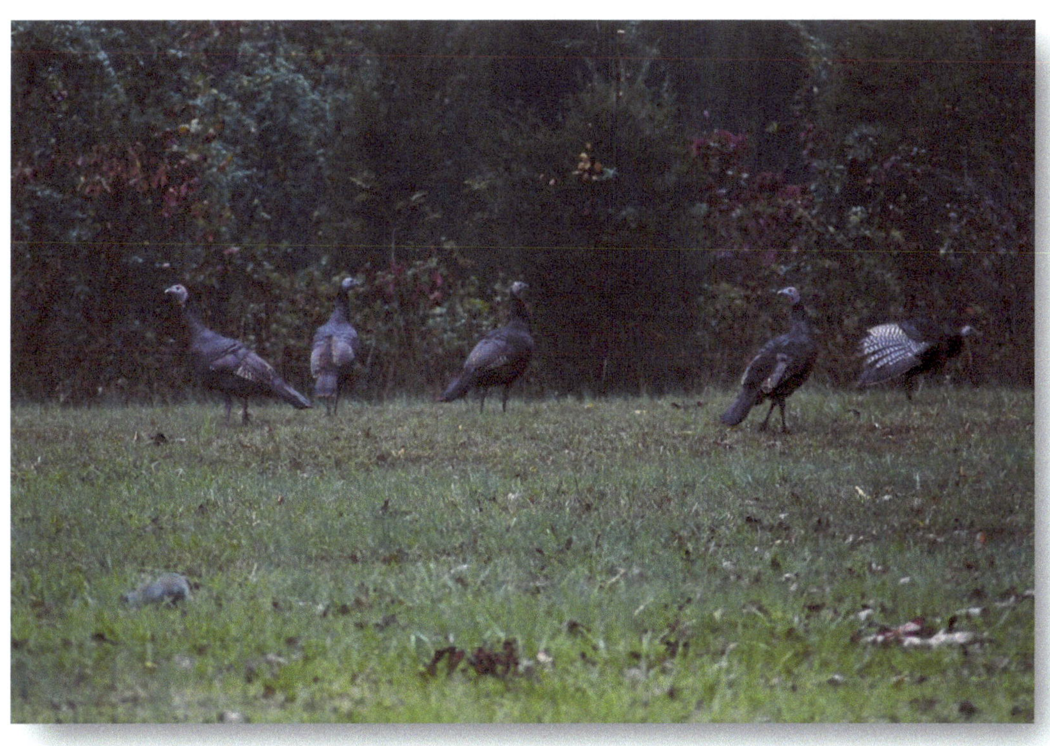

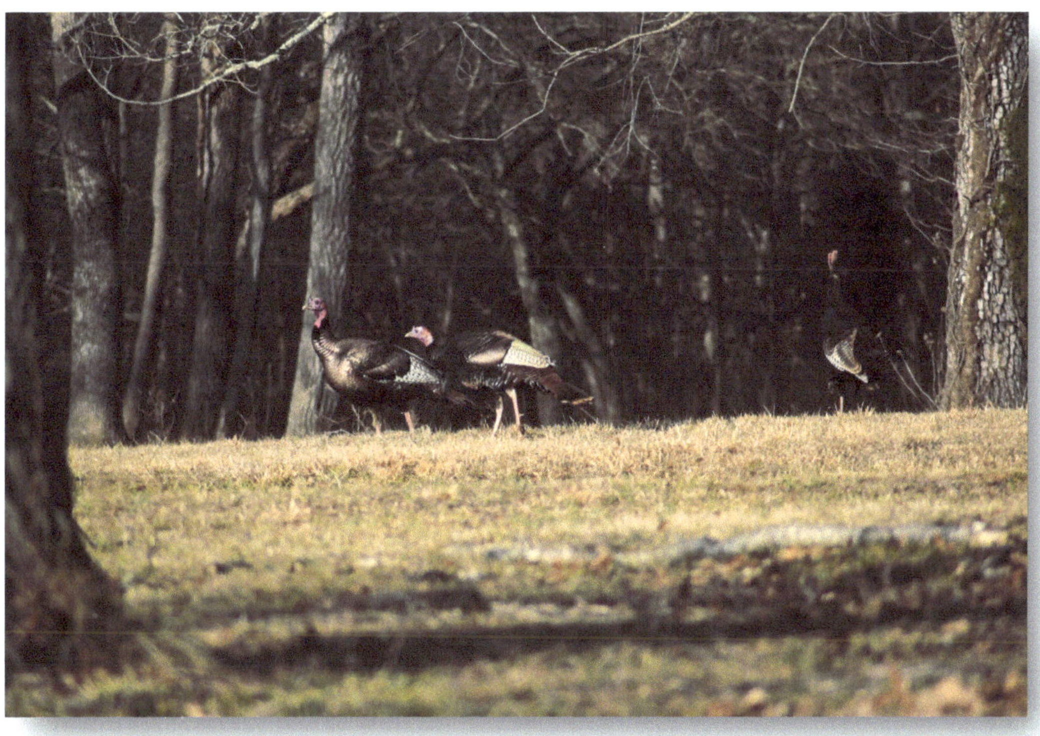

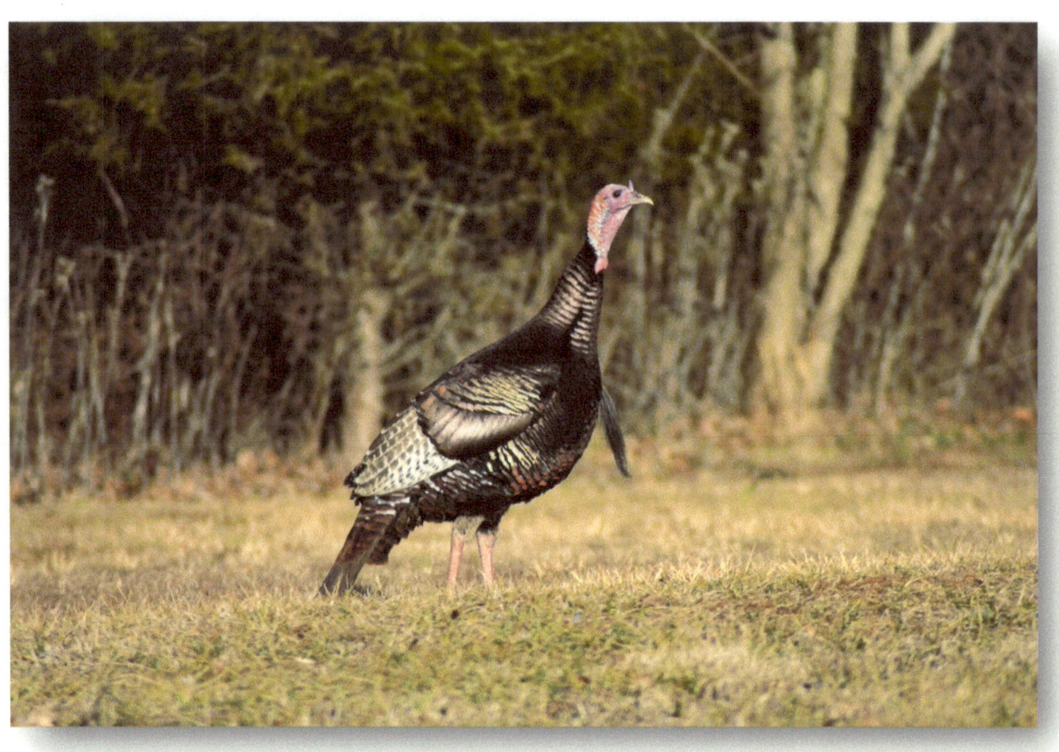

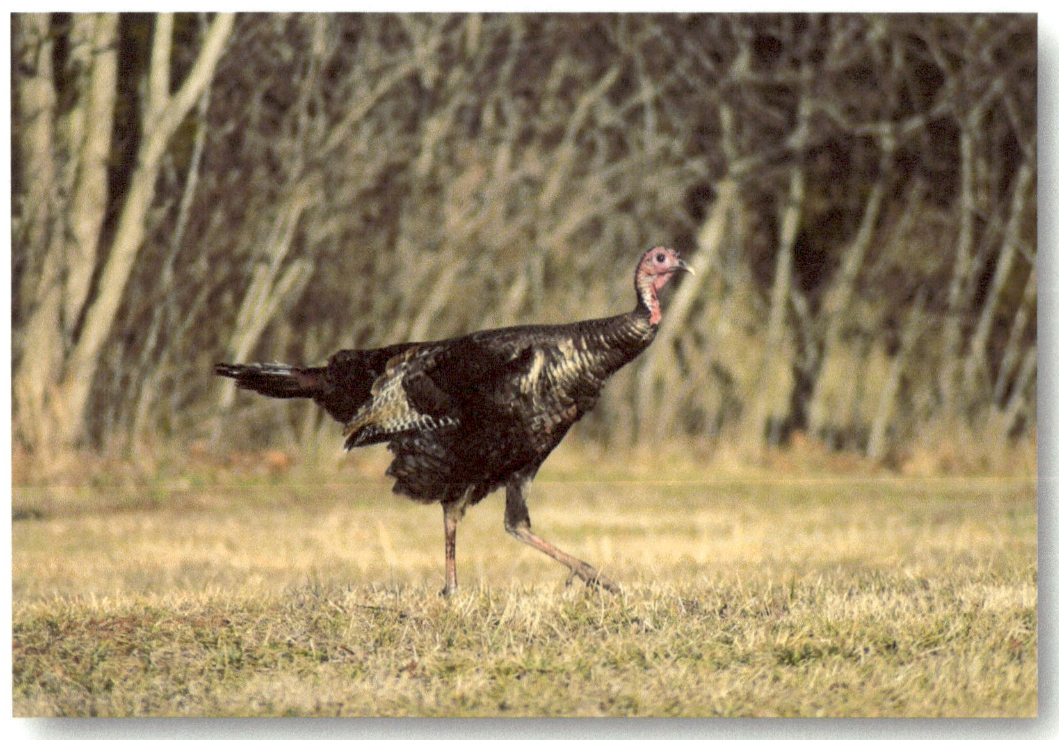

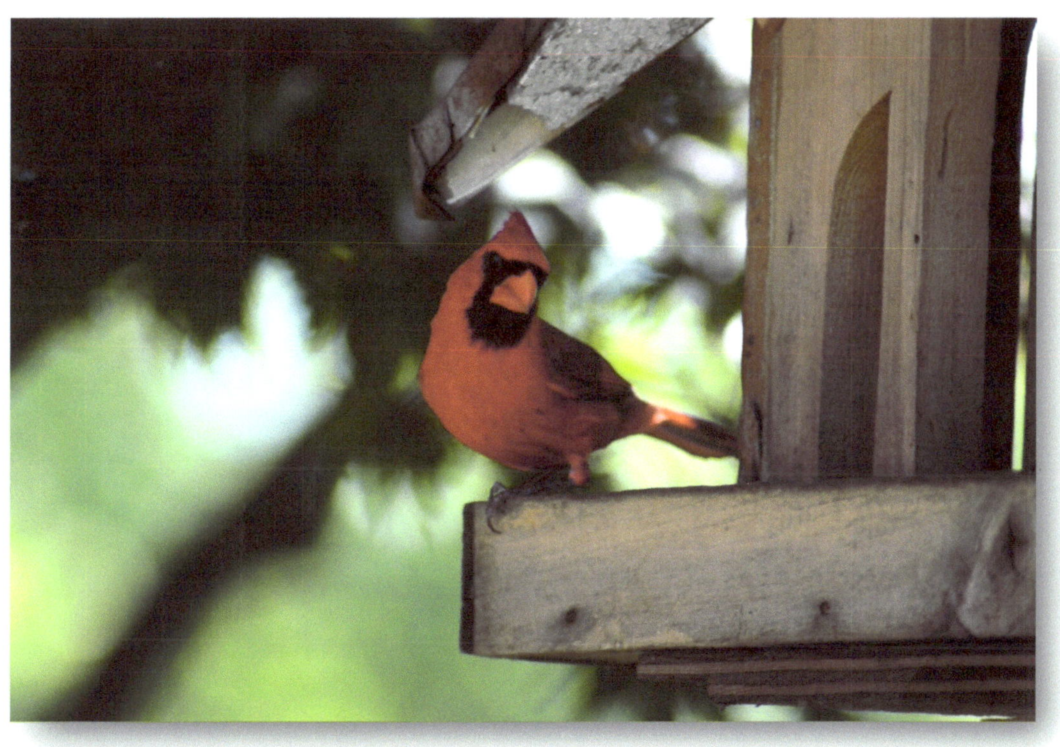

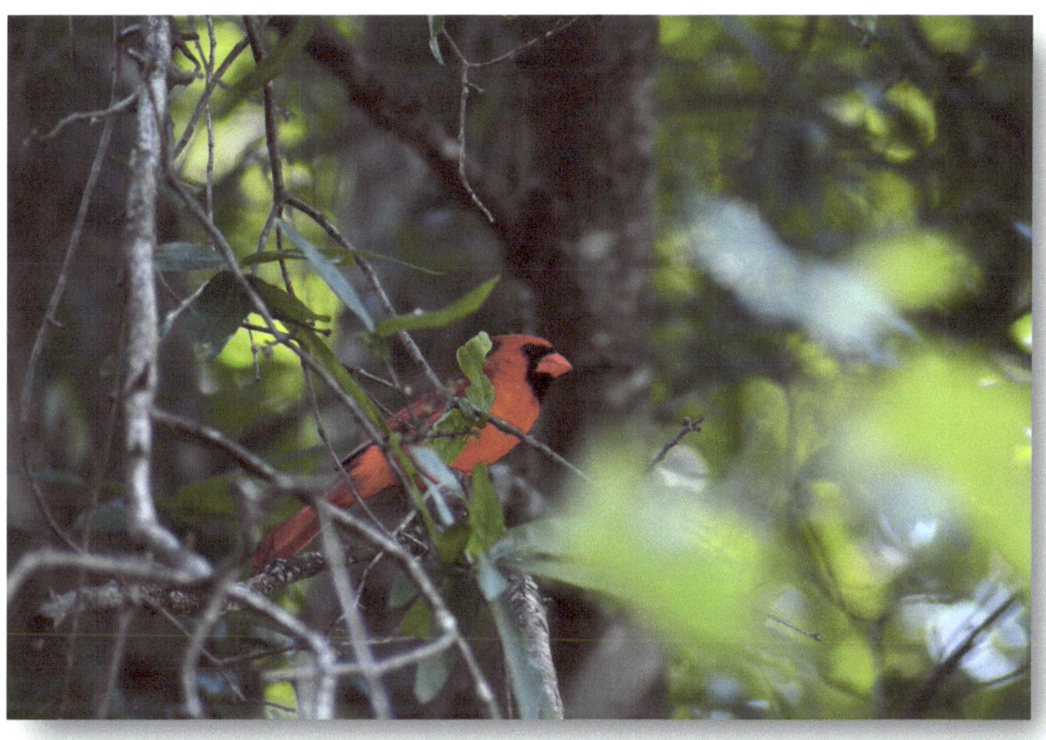

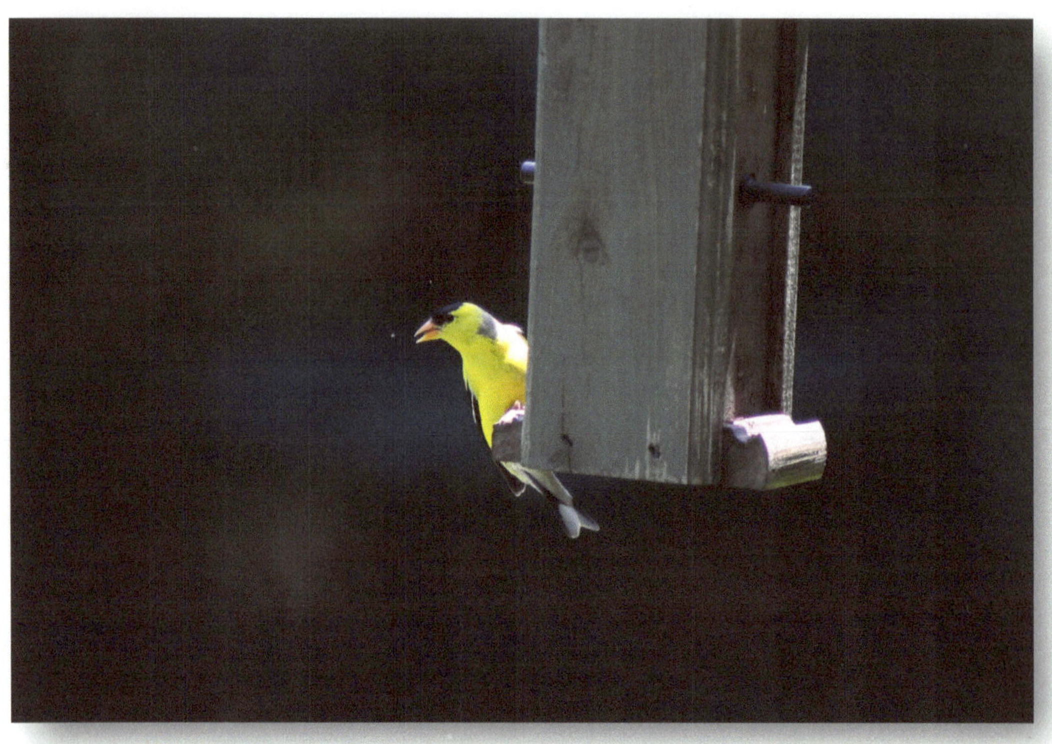

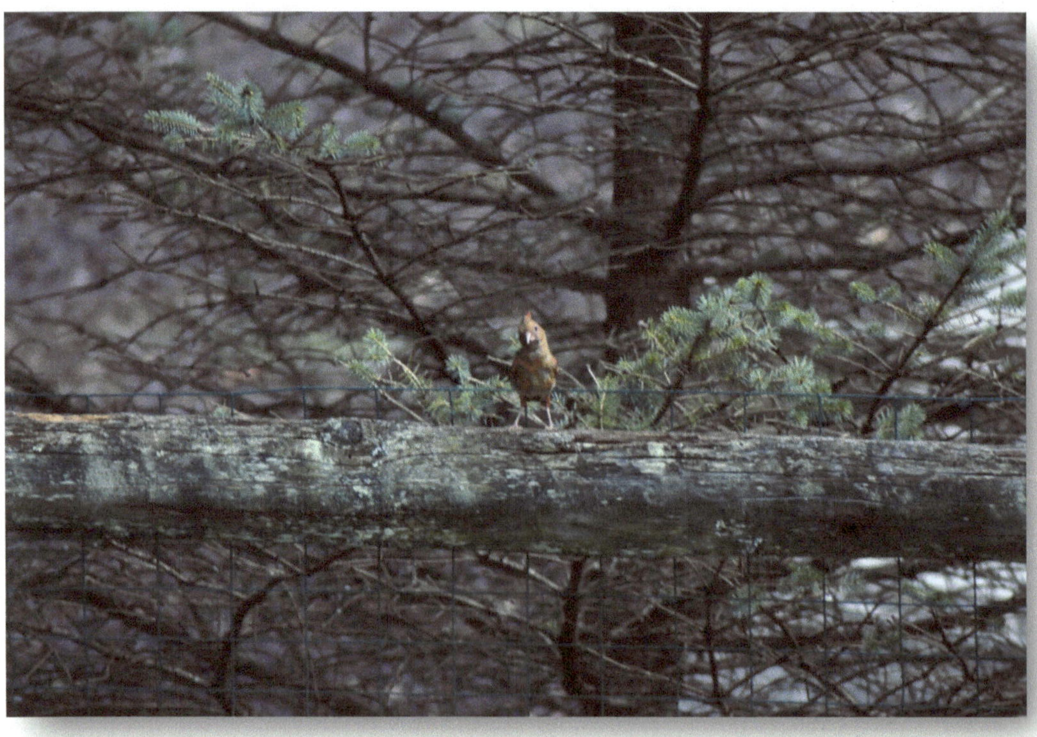

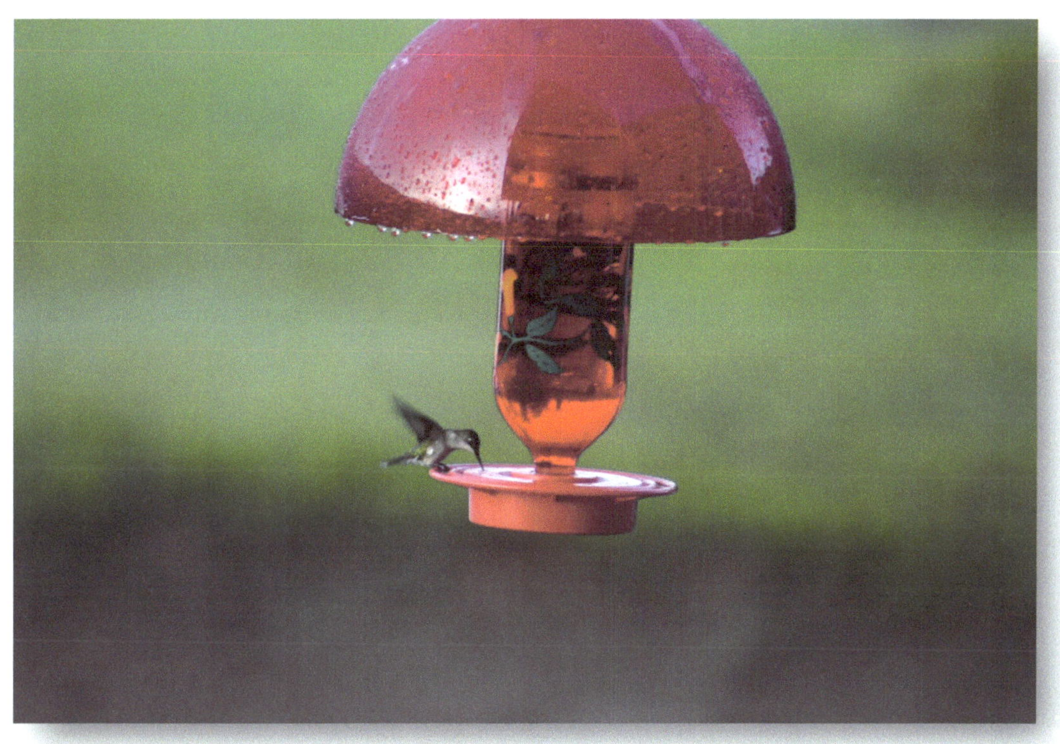

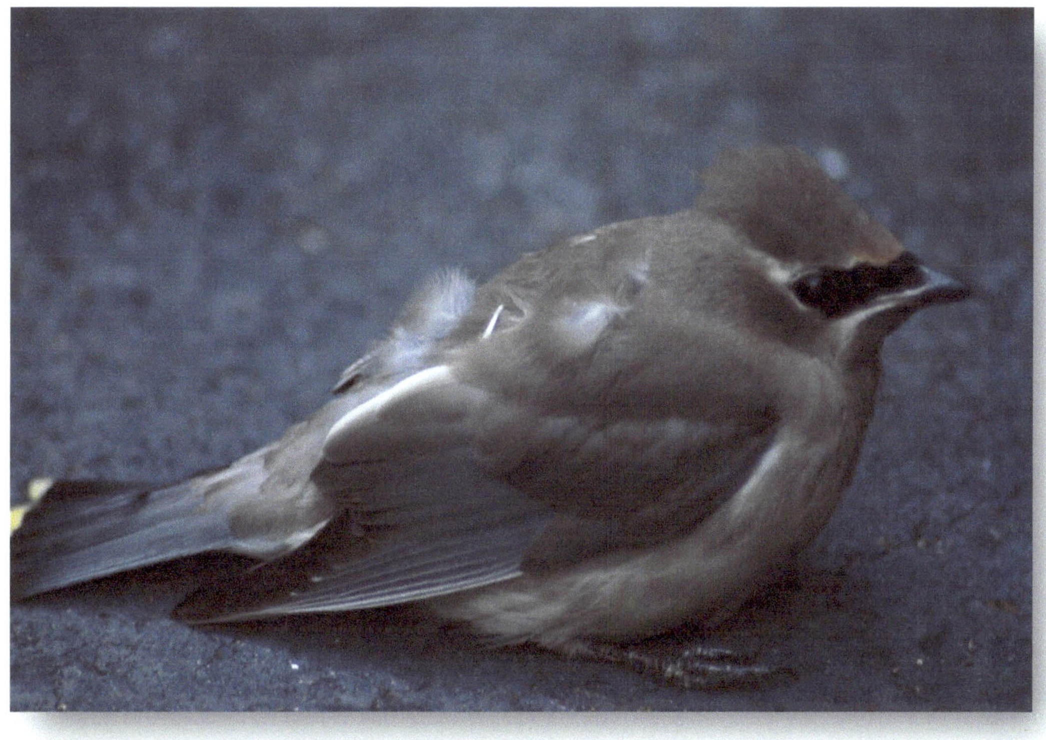

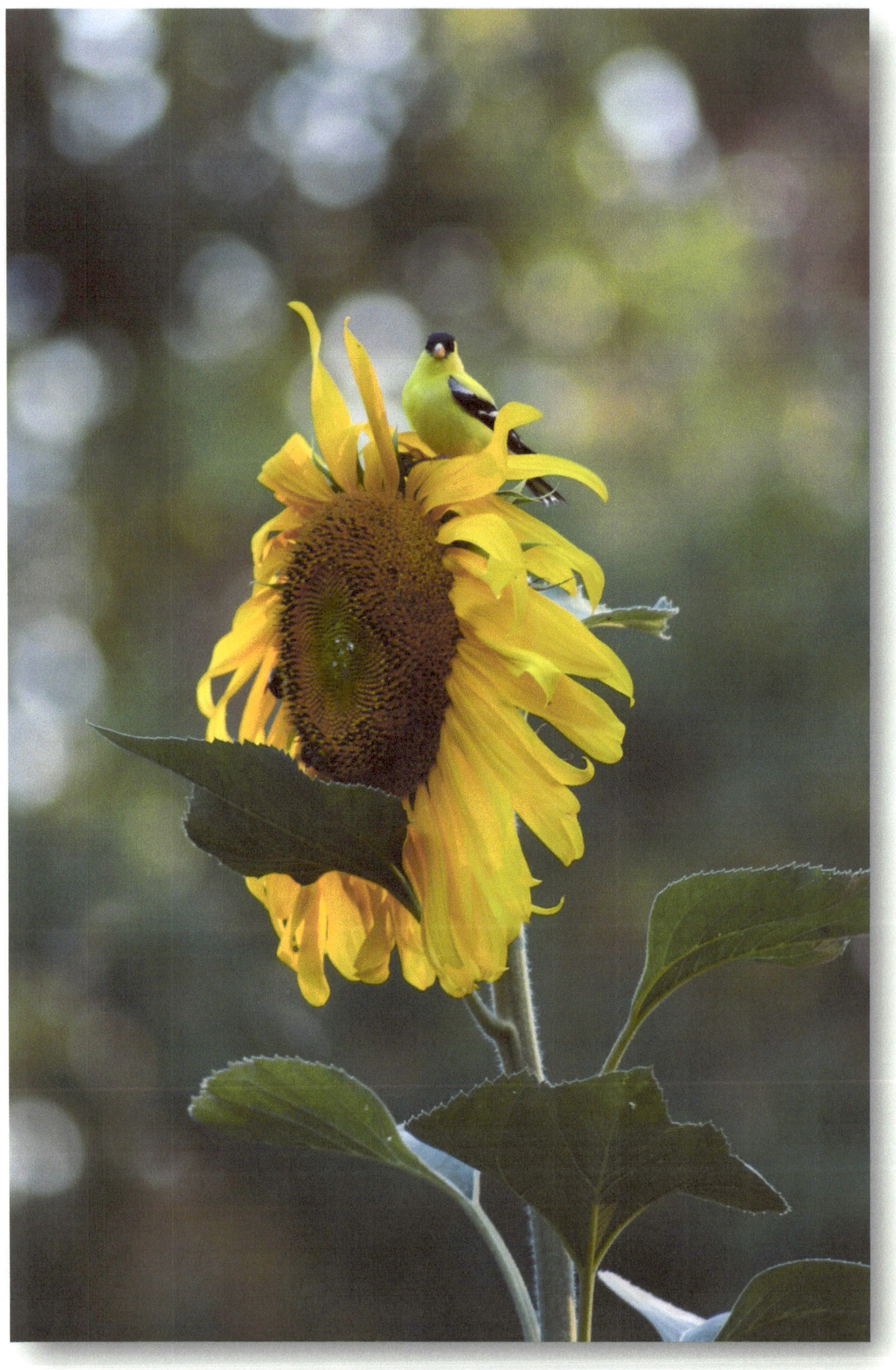

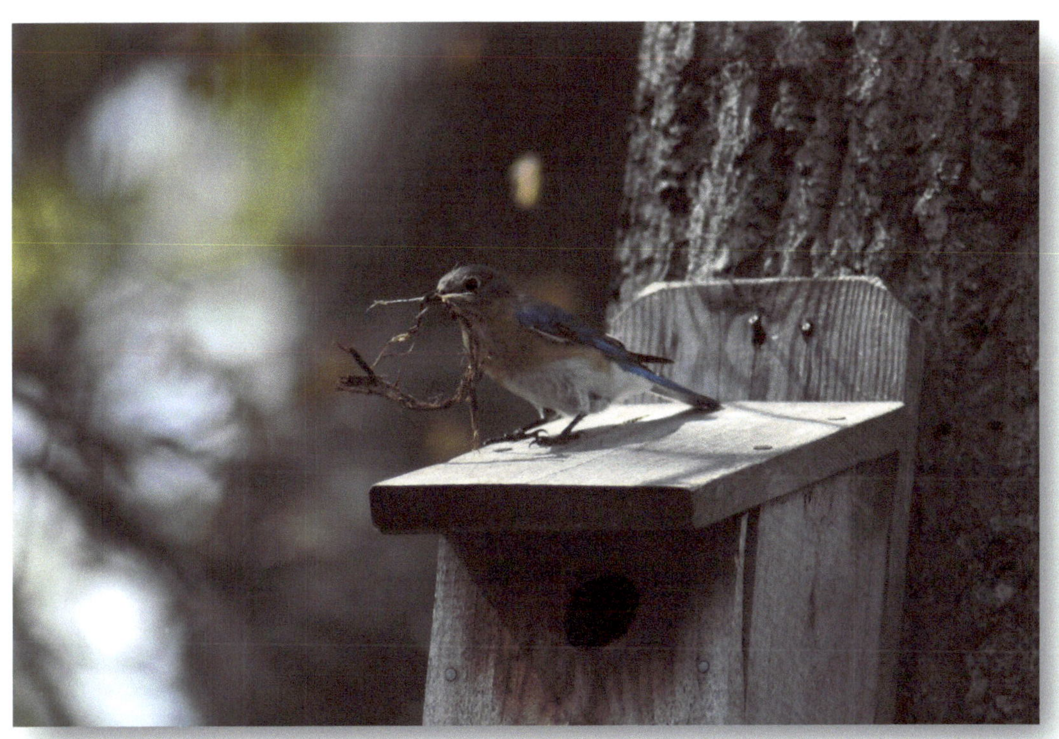

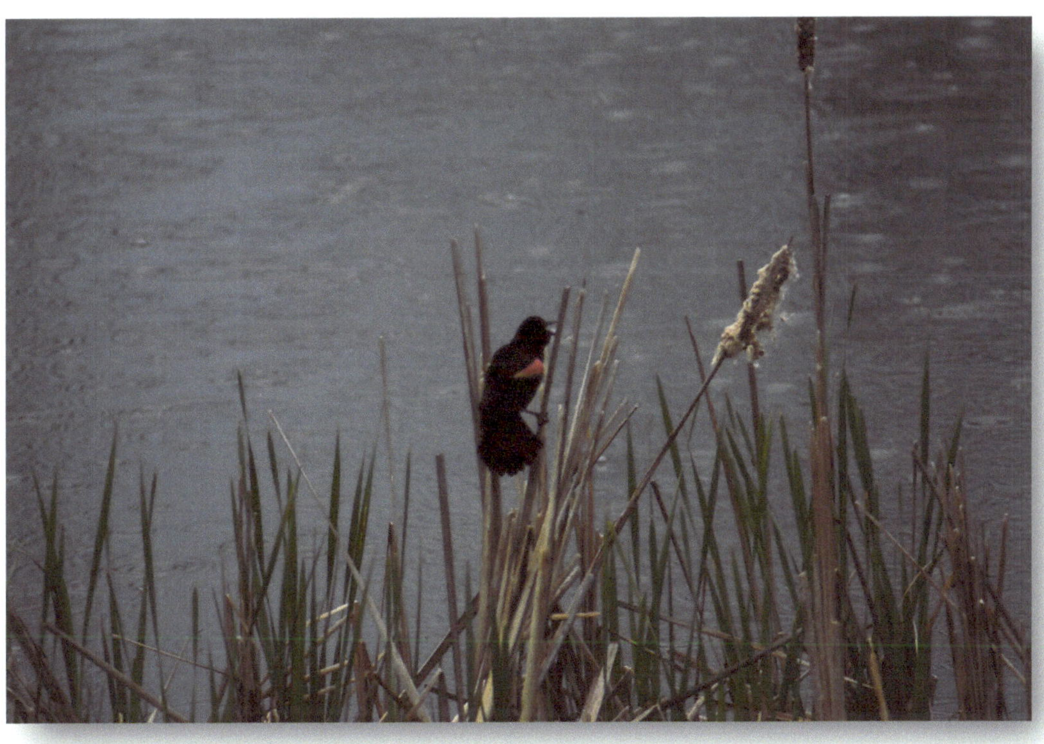

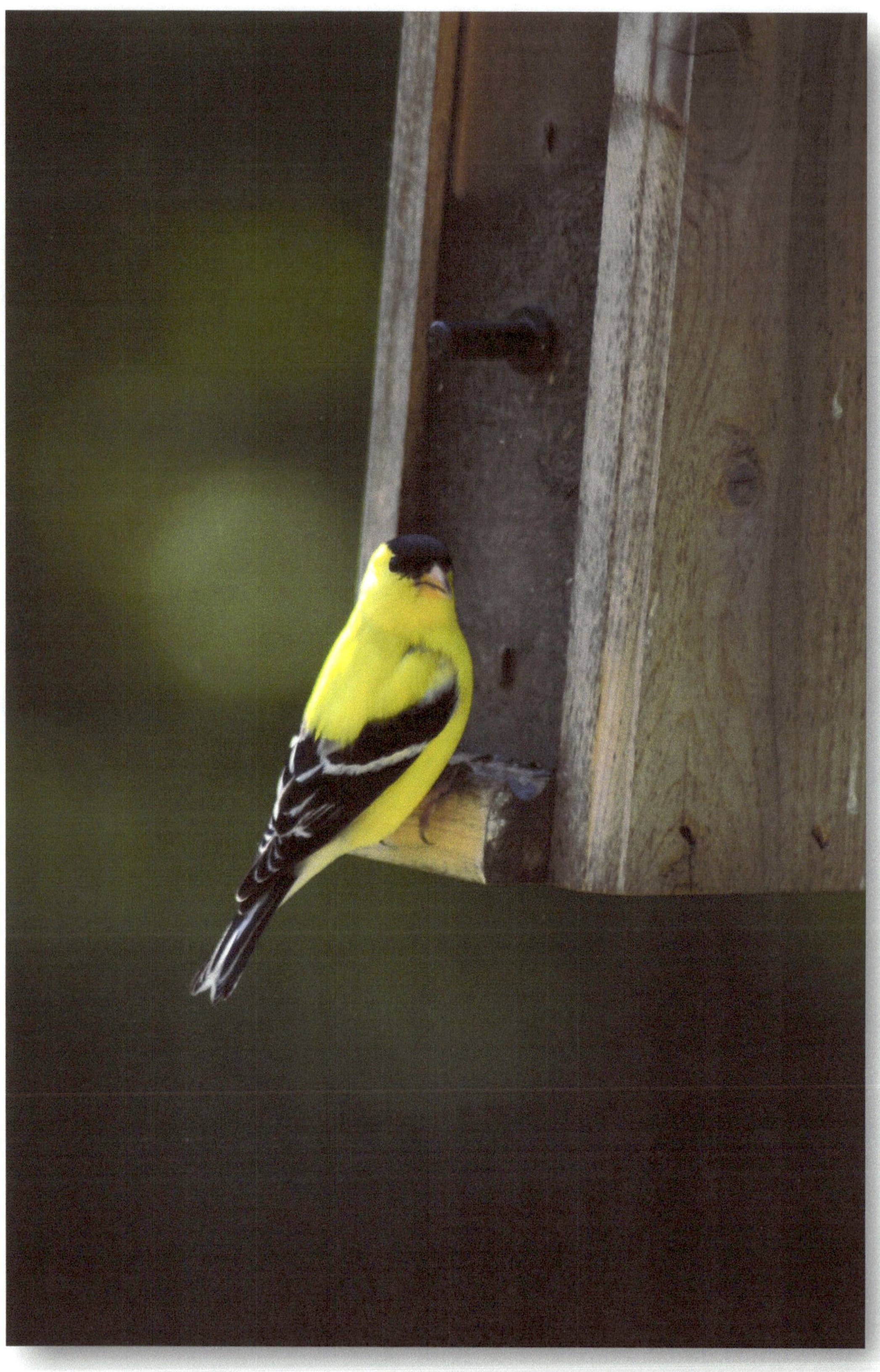

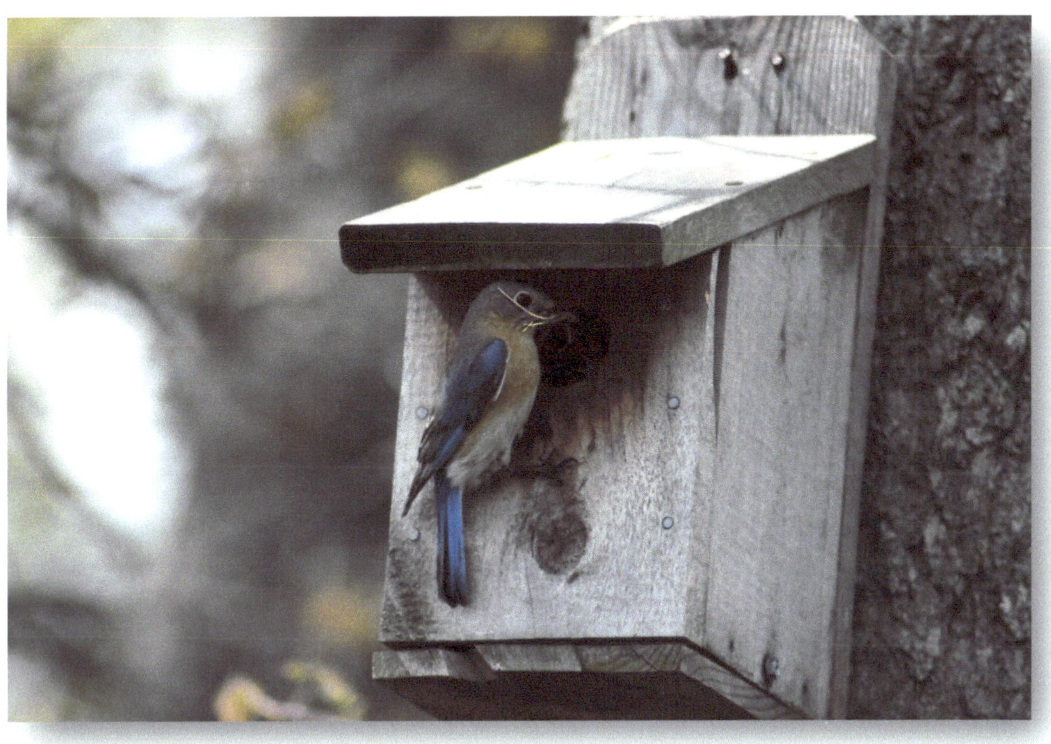

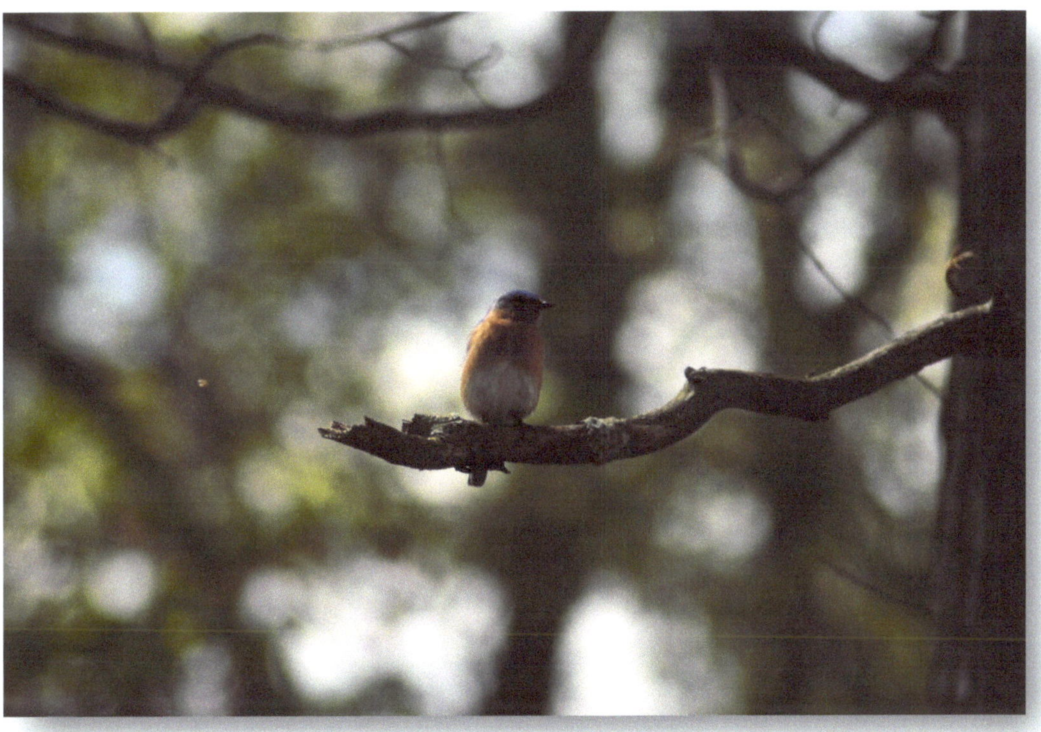

About the Photographer

Tracey Yvette Hughes was born in Halifax, Virginia and was raised in Campbell County, Virginia. She is a devoted mother of two smart and pretty teenage daughters. Tracey attended college at University of California, Northridge and high school at William Campbell High School. She loves the outdoors and enjoys capturing those shots of rare moments in nature. Tracey now lives in Lynchburg, Virginia.

From an early age, Tracey started snapping photos of everything. As a young adult, she began to focus more on quality shots of landscape, flowers, wildlife and portraits in natural settings.

The pictures in this book were taken in Virginia. Most were photographed in Bedford and Campbell counties.

Other books by Tracey are available, including ***Virginia Flowers***. Check the Deep Sea Publishing website for ordering details.

Deep Sea Publishing

Deep Sea Publishing, LLC is a Florida company with offices in Florida and Virginia. The company publishes:

- Fictional Novels,
- Historical Fiction,
- Children's Books,
- Young Adult and Teen Fiction,
- Technical References,
- Photography Books,
- and more.

Deep Sea Publishing is a USA firm owned by 100% USA citizens. All printing and production is in the USA. Other works from Deep Sea Publishing include:

- ***The Bryant Family Chronicles: Death and Gold in Zara Zote***
- ***The Gallivan Legacy***
- ***Hardt's Tale***
- ***Let Sleeping Dragons Lie***
- ***The Good Fight***
- ***Seven Summits: The Magical Talent***
- ***Not Myself***
- ***Carcharhinus obscurus, & Carcharias Taurus (kids' shark books)***
- ***My Seasons with Grandma Francesca and Grandma Louise (children's book)***
- ***Christmas in Paradise (children's book).***

To find out more about Deep Sea Publishing or to order books, visit our website at www.deepseapublishing.com.

www.ingramcontent.com/pod-product-compliance
Lightning Source LLC
LaVergne TN
LVHW070152110826
845147LV00002B/382

* 9 7 8 1 9 3 9 5 3 5 0 2 3 *